"In this book Paul Cra[...]  nany
unpopular truths that [...]

— RALPH GOMORY, PF[...]
  SLOAN FOUNDATION

"Roberts combines the technical understanding of a
PhD economist, the political savvy of a former Assistant
Secretary of the Treasury, the clear focused brevity of a
practiced journalist, and the passion of a patriotic citizen
angered at the plunder of our country by a greedy elite.
Highly recommended!"

— HERMAN E. DALY, FORMER WORLD BANK ECONOMIST
  AND PROFESSOR OF PUBLIC POLICY,
  UNIVERSITY OF MARYLAND.

"Paul Craig Roberts draws attention to the most egregious
policy errors the government continues to make every
month. He makes it clear that the structure itself needs
to be changed, not just the execution of fundamentally
misguided policies."

— MICHAEL HUDSON, ECONOMIST,
  AUTHOR OF *Super Imperialism.*

"Paul Craig Roberts has looked at U.S. monetary policy
from the inside, as former Assistant Secretary of the
Treasury, and from the outside, currently as a repulsed
citizen and journalist. As he sounds the alarm on the U.S.
financial trajectory, policymakers need to pay attention."

— PAM MARTENS, FORMER WALL ST FINANCIAL ANALYST.

HOW THE

ECONOMY

WAS LOST

PART ONE

The Lost Economy

PART TWO

War of the Worlds

First published by
CounterPunch and AK Press 2010

CounterPunch
PO Box 228, Petrolia, California 95558

AK Press
674-A 23rd St, Oakland, California 94612-1163

ISBN 978-1849350075

A catalog record for this book is available from the Library of Congress.
Library of Congress Control Number: 2009907357

Typeset in Minion Pro, designed by Robert Slimbach for Adobe Systems Inc.;
and Futura, originally designed by Paul Renner.

Printed and bound in Canada.

Design and typography by Tiffany Wardle de Sousa.

HOW THE
ECONOMY
WAS LOST

PAUL CRAIG ROBERTS

CounterPunch
PETROLIA

Contents

Introduction

N THE FIRST DECADE OF THE 21ST CENTURY AMERICANS HAVE experienced the worst economy since the Great Depression of the 1930s. Today's policy-makers are just as bereft of solutions as policy-makers 80 years ago. More Americans have lost their homes in the current crisis than during the Great Depression. In some states the unemployment rate is already at Great Depression levels even as the current crisis continues to develop. Tent cities are again appearing.

The Great Depression lasted for a decade, because its cause was not understood. As policy-makers did not understand the cause of the problem, they could not formulate a solution, and the suffering was prolonged.

As an economist and a columnist watching the current crisis develop and unfold, I have endeavored to explain what is occurring in order that course corrections can be made and the worst avoided. The first part of this book is a collection of columns published by *CounterPunch* over the past five years that explain what is happening to us and why.

The columns deal with a range of issues that are vital to understanding our situation: how jobs offshoring erodes Americans' employment prospects, dismantles the ladders of upward mobility, and worsens the income distribution; how offshoring increases the trade and budget deficits and creates financing problems for the U.S. government that threaten the dollar's role as world reserve currency, the main basis of U.S. power; how necessary changes in economic policy are blocked by organized special interests who spin explanations designed to further their own agendas; how deregulation permitted debt leverage to exceed any measure of prudence.

Being the reserve currency country allows the U.S. government to escape trade and budget discipline, because the U.S. can pay for its imports in its own currency. There is no discipline to match imports with exports in order to earn the foreign currencies with which to pay the import bill. Thus, the trade deficit tends to grow continuously.

Indeed, there is a tendency for government to see the trade deficit in a positive light as it provides foreigners with dollars that they recycle by purchasing U.S. Treasury debt, thus financing the U.S. government's budget deficits.

The U.S. government's policy of benign neglect of the trade deficit has permitted the trade deficit to reach unsustainable levels. This has occurred simultaneously with the federal budget deficit reaching unsustainable levels. Enlarged by the bank bailout, the stimulus package, expensive wars, and the loss of tax revenues to the deteriorating economy, the federal budget deficits for fiscal years 2009 and 2010 will each be four times larger than the 2008 deficit. Financing needs for 2009 and 2010 come to $3 trillion according to current estimates.

The unanswered question is: who has $3 trillion to lend to Washington? The sum is far larger than the trade surpluses of our trading partners, so the traditional recycling will not cover the red ink. Americans are deep in debt and lack the means to purchase the government's debt. The danger is that the government will resort to printing money in order to pay its bills.

This would add inflation, perhaps hyperinflation, to high unemployment and present government with a crisis for which economic policy has no solution. It would place the political stability of the United States in doubt.

So far into the crisis, the Obama administration and most economists regard the problem as a credit problem. Banks, impaired by questionable investments in derivatives, can't lend. Economists believe that the solution is to restart the credit cycle by using taxpayers' money, or money borrowed abroad, to take the bad investments off the banks' hands. This solution overlooks the fact that consumers are so overloaded with debt that they cannot afford to borrow more in order to finance more consumption.

The essays in Part One explain why piling debt upon debt is not a solution to problems caused by moving American middle class jobs abroad. The real incomes of Americans ceased to grow in the 21st century, because many of the jobs that produce real income gains have been moved offshore. An increase in consumer indebtedness substituted for growth in real incomes and sustained the growth of the economy until mortgage and credit card debts reached their limits.

The essays in Part One explain why fiscal stimulus—a larger budget deficit—is part of the problem, not part of the solution.

Obama's policy, like Bush's before him, is on the wrong track. If the course is not changed, the crash will be hard indeed.

There is repetition in the chapters, because the government's statistics over the years consistently support the point that the US economy is ceasing to create middle class jobs. The mounting evidence, reported in my columns, is important. We have spent a decade losing middle class jobs while economists sing the praise of the "New Economy." Likewise, the dollar has continued to lose value in relation to other hard currencies.

Part Two offers in ordinary language a short course in economics keyed to the unrecognized problems of our time. A widespread misunderstanding of free trade by policy-makers and economists has resulted in free trade becoming an excuse for the erosion of the productive capability of the American economy. Free trade has a hallowed status among most economists. Consequently, it is an unexamined article of faith. Economists even believe that jobs offshoring is a manifestation of free trade and, thus, a benefit to the U.S. economy.

In Chapters 49 and 50 I explain the unacknowledged problems in free trade doctrine and why jobs offshoring is not free trade.

In Chapter 51, I explain the fundamental error in economists' assumption that natural resources are inexhaustible. This uninformed assumption permits nature's capital to be exhausted with no thought to the consequences. On this point, the failure of economic thinking is so great as to call into question the designation of economics as a science.

The final two chapters explain how businesses maximize profits by imposing costs on others and how we might mitigate these costs. Economists term these imposed costs "external costs." In a "full world" (see Chapter 51), external costs might be the greatest part of costs. Have we reached a stage in capitalist development in which a large, and perhaps the major, cost of capitalist profits are imposed on third parties who do not share in the profits? In the U.S. today, corporate profits are no longer related to the welfare of the general population as corporations maximize their profits by replacing American labor with foreign labor.

In the presence of powerful organized special interests, does representative government have sufficient independence and integrity to represent the public interest?

This is the unanswered question.

If the American people wish to continue as a viable society, they must inform themselves of their plight and demand change. If they acquiesce in propaganda and disinformation from the special interests who are enriched by America's decline—the same special interests that control their government—the bulk of the American population is headed for Third World status.

This book is my contribution to my fellow citizens' welfare. Wake up! Be aware that the interest groups that control "your" government are destroying you.

PAUL CRAIG ROBERTS
NOVEMBER 8, 2009

PART ONE

The Lost Economy

CHAPTER 1

The Return of the Robber Barons

THE U.S. ECONOMY CONTINUES ITS 21ST CENTURY DECLINE, EVEN AS the Bush Regime outfits B-2 stealth bombers with 30,000 pound monster "bunker buster" bombs for a possible attack on Iran. While profits soar for the armaments industry, the American people continue to take it on the chin.

The latest report from the Bureau of Labor Statistics shows that the real wages and salaries of U.S. civilian workers are below those of five years ago. It could not be otherwise with U.S. corporations offshoring good jobs in order to reduce labor costs and, thereby, to convert wages once paid to Americans into multi-million dollar bonuses paid to CEOs and other top management.

Good jobs that still remain in the U.S. are increasingly filled with foreign workers brought in on work visas. Corporate public relations departments have successfully spread the lie that there is a shortage of qualified U.S. workers, necessitating the importation into the U.S. of foreigners. The truth is that the U.S. corporations force their American employees to train the lower paid foreigners who take their jobs. Otherwise, the discharged American gets no severance pay.

Law firms, such as Cohen & Grigsby, compete in marketing their services to U.S. corporations on how to evade the law and to replace their American employees with lower paid foreigners. As Lawrence Lebowitz, vice president at Cohen & Grigsby, explained in the law firm's marketing video, "our goal is, clearly, not to find a qualified and interested U.S. worker."

Meanwhile, U.S. colleges and universities continue to graduate hundreds of thousands of qualified engineers, IT professionals, and other professionals who will never have the opportunity to work in the professions for which they have been trained. America today is like India of yesteryear, with engineers working as bartenders, taxi cab drivers, waitresses, and employed in menial work in dog kennels as the offshoring of U.S. jobs dismantles the ladders of upward mobility for U.S. citizens.

Over the last year (from June 2006 through June 2007) the U.S. economy created 1.6 million net private sector jobs. Essentially all of the new jobs are in low-paid domestic services that do not require a college education.

The category, "leisure and hospitality," accounts for 30 per cent of the new jobs, of which 387,000 are bartenders and waitresses, 38,000 are workers in motels and hotels, and 50,000 are employed in entertainment and recreation.

The category, "education and health services," accounts for 35 per cent of the gain in employment, of which 100,000 are in educational services and 456,000 are in health care and social assistance, principally ambulatory health care services and hospitals. There is much evidence that many teaching and nursing jobs are being filled by foreigners brought in on work visas.

"Professional and technical services" accounts for 268,000 of the new jobs. "Finance and insurance" added 93,000 new jobs, of which about one quarter are in real estate and about one half are in insurance. "Transportation and warehousing" added 65,000 jobs, and wholesale and retail trade added 185,000.

Over the entire year, the U.S. economy created merely 51,000 jobs in architectural and engineering services, less than the 76,000 jobs created in management and technical consulting (essentially laid-off white collar professionals). Except for a well-connected few graduates, who find their way into Wall Street investment banks, top law firms, and private medical practice, American universities today consist of detention centers to delay for four or five years the entry of American youth into unskilled domestic services.

Meanwhile the rich are getting much richer and luxuriating in the most fantastic conspicuous consumption since the Gilded Age. Robert Frank has dubbed the new American world of the super-rich "Richistan."

In Richistan there is a two-year waiting list for $50 million 200-foot yachts. In Richistan Rolex watches are considered Wal-Mart junk. Richistanians sport $736,000 Franck Muller timepieces, sign their names with $700,000 Mont Blanc jewel-encrusted pens. Their valets, butlers (with $100,000 salaries), and bodyguards carry the $42,000 Louis Vuitton handbags of wives and mistresses.

Richistanians join clubs open only to those with $100 million, pay $650,000 for golf club memberships, eat $50 hamburgers and $1,000 omelettes, drink $90 a bottle Bling mineral water and down $10,000 "martinis on a rock" (gin or vodka poured over a diamond) at New York's Algonquin Hotel.

Who are the Richistanians? They are CEOs who have moved their companies abroad and converted the wages they formerly paid Americans into $100 million compensation packages for themselves. They are investment bankers and hedge fund managers, who created the subprime mortgage derivatives that threaten to collapse the economy. One of them was paid $1.7 billion last year. The $575 million that each of the 25 other top earners were paid is paltry by comparison, but unimaginable wealth to everyone else.

Some of the super rich, such as Warren Buffet and Bill Gates, have benefitted society along with themselves. Both Buffet and Gates are concerned about the rapidly rising income inequality in the U.S. They are aware that America is becoming a feudal society in which the super-rich compete in conspicuous consumption, while the serfs struggle merely to survive.

With the real wages and salaries of American civilian workers lower than five years ago, with their debts at all time highs, with the prices of their main asset—their homes—under pressure from overbuilding and fraudulent finance, and with scant opportunities to rise for the children they struggled to educate, Americans face a dim future. Indeed, their plight is worse than the official statistics indicate. During the Clinton administration, the Boskin Commission rigged the inflation measures in order to hold down indexed Social Security payments to retirees.

Another deceit is the measure called "core inflation." This measure of inflation excludes food and energy, two large components of the average family's budget. Wall Street and corporations and, therefore, the media emphasize core inflation, because it holds down cost of living increases and interest rates. In the second quarter of this year, the Consumer

Price Index (CPI), a more complete measure of inflation, increased at an annual rate of 5.2 per cent compared to 2.3 per cent for core inflation.

An examination of how inflation is measured quickly reveals the games played to deceive the American people. Housing prices are not in the index. Instead, the rental rate of housing is used as a proxy for housing prices.

More games are played with the goods and services whose prices comprise the weighted market basket used to estimate inflation. If beef prices rise, for example, the index shifts toward lower priced cuts. Inflation is thus held down by substituting lower priced products for those whose prices are rising more. As the weights of the goods in the basket change, the inflation measure does not reflect a constant pattern of expenditures. Some economists compare the substitution used to minimize the measured rate of inflation to substituting sweaters for fuel oil.

Other deceptions, not all intentional, abound in official U.S. statistics. *Business Week*'s June 18, 2007 cover story used the recent important work by Susan N. Houseman to explain that much of the hyped gains in U.S. productivity and GDP are "phantom gains" that are not really there.

Other phantom productivity gains are produced by corporations that shift business costs to consumers by, for example, having callers listen to advertisements while they wait for a customer service representative, and by the government pricing items in the inflation basket according to the low prices of stores that offer customers no service. The longer callers can be made to wait, the fewer the customer representatives the company needs to employ. The loss of service is not considered in the inflation measure. It shows up instead as a gain in productivity.

In America today the greatest rewards go to investment bankers, who collect fees for creating financing packages for debt. These packages include the tottering subprime mortgage derivatives. Recently, a top official of the Bank of France acknowledged that the real values of repackaged debt instruments are unknown to both buyers and sellers. Many of the derivatives have never been priced by the market.

Think of derivatives as a mutual fund of debt, a combination of good mortgages, subprime mortgages, credit card debt, auto loans, and who knows what. Not even institutional buyers know what they are buying or how to evaluate it. Arcane pricing models are used to produce values, and pay incentives bias the assigned values upward.

Richistan wealth may prove artificial and crash, bringing an end to the new Gilded Age. But the plight of the rich in distress will never compare to the decimation of America's middle class. The offshoring of American jobs has destroyed opportunities for generations of Americans.

Never before in our history has the elite had such control over the government. To run for national office requires many millions of dollars, the raising of which puts "our" elected representatives and "our" president himself at the beck and call of the few moneyed interests that financed the campaigns.

America as the land of opportunity has passed away into history.

AUGUST 2, 2007

CHAPTER 2

Greenspan and the Economy of Greed

FORMER FED CHAIRMAN ALAN GREENSPAN'S MEMOIR HAS PUT him in the news these last few days. He has upset Republicans with his comments on various presidents, with George W. Bush getting the brickbats and Clinton the praise, and by saying that Bush's invasion of Iraq was about oil, not weapons of mass destruction.

Opponents of Bush's wars welcomed Greenspan's statement, as it strips the moral pretext away from Bush's aggression, leaving naked greed unmasked.

It is certainly the case that Iraq was not invaded because of WMD, which the Bush administration knew did not exist. But the oil pretext is also phony. The U.S. could have purchased a lot of oil for the trillion dollars that the Iraq invasion has already cost in out-of-pocket expenses and already incurred future expenses.

Moreover, Bush's invasion of Iraq, by worsening the U.S. deficit and causing additional U.S. reliance on foreign loans, has undermined the U.S. dollar's role as reserve currency, thus threatening America's ability to pay for its imports. Greenspan himself said that the U.S. dollar "doesn't have all that much of an advantage" and could be replaced by the Euro as the reserve currency. By the end of last year, Greenspan said, foreign central banks already held 25 per cent of their reserves in Euros and 9 per cent in other foreign currencies. The dollar's role has shrunk to 66 per cent.

If the dollar loses its reserve currency status, the U.S. would magically have to move from an $800 billion trade deficit to a trade surplus so that the U.S. could earn enough Euros to pay for its imports of oil and manufactured goods and settle its current account deficit.

Bush's wars are about American hegemony, not oil. The oil companies did not write the neoconservatives' "Project for a New American Century," which calls for U.S./Israeli hegemony over the entire Middle

East, a hegemony that would conveniently remove obstacles to Israeli territorial expansion.

The oil industry asserted its influence after the invasion. In his book, *Armed Madhouse*, BBC investigative reporter Greg Palast documents that the U.S. oil industry's interest in Middle Eastern oil is very different from grabbing the oil. Palast shows that the American oil companies' interests coincide with OPEC's. The oil companies want a controlled flow of oil that results in steady and high prices. Consequently, the U.S. oil industry blocked the neoconservative plan, hatched at the Heritage Foundation and aimed at Saudi Arabia, to use Iraqi oil to bust up OPEC.

Saddam Hussein got in trouble because one moment he would cut production to support the Palestinians and the next moment he would pump the maximum allowed. Up and down movements in prices are destabilizing events for the oil industry. Palast reports that a Council on Foreign Relations report concludes: Saddam is a "destabilizing influence . . . to the flow of oil to international markets from the Middle East."

The most notable aspect of Greenspan's memoir is his unconcern with America's loss of manufacturing. Instead of a problem, Greenspan simply sees a beneficial shift in jobs from "old" manufacturing (steel, cars, and textiles) to "new" manufacturing such as computers and tele-communications. This shows a remarkable ignorance of statistical data on the part of a Federal Reserve Chairman renowned for his command over numbers and a complete lack of grasp of offshoring.

The incentive to offshore U.S. jobs has nothing to do with "old" and "new" economy. Corporations offshore their production, because they can more cheaply produce abroad what they sell to Americans. When corporations bring their offshored production to the U.S. to sell, the goods count as imports.

Had Greenspan bothered to look at U.S. balance of trade data, he would have discovered that in 2006, the last full year of data (at time of writing), the U.S. exported $47,580,000,000 in computers and imported $101,347,000,000 in computers for a trade deficit in computers of $53,767,000,000. In telecommunications equipment the U.S. exported $28,322,000,000 and imported $40,250,000,000 for a trade deficit in telecommunications equipment of $11,883,000,000.

Greenspan probably has given offshoring no serious thought, because like most economists he mistakenly believes that offshoring is free trade and learned in economic courses decades ago before the advent of offshoring that free trade can do no harm.

For most of the 21st century I have been pointing out that offshoring is not trade, free or otherwise. It is labor arbitrage. By replacing U.S. labor with foreign labor in the production of goods and services for U.S. markets, U.S. firms are destroying the ladders of upward mobility in the U.S. So far economists have preferred their delusions to the facts.

It is becoming more difficult for economists to clutch to their bosoms the delusion that offshoring is free trade. Ralph Gomory, the distinguished mathematician and co-author with William Baumol (past president of the American Economics Association) of *Global Trade and Conflicting National Interests*, the most important work in trade theory in 200 years, has entered the public debate.

In an interview with *Manufacturing & Technology News* (September 17), Gomory confirms that there is no basis in economic theory for claiming that it is good to tear down our own productive capability and to rebuild it in a foreign country. It is not free trade when a company relocates its manufacturing abroad.

Gomory says that economists and policymakers "still are treating companies as if they represent the country, and they do not." Companies are no longer bound to the interests of their home countries, because the link has been decoupled between the profit motive and a country's welfare. Economists, Gomory points out, are not acknowledging the implications of this decoupling for economic theory.

A country that offshores its own production is unable to balance its trade. Americans are able to consume more than they produce only because the dollar is the world reserve currency. However, the dollar's reserve currency status is eroded by the debts associated with continual trade and budget deficits.

The U.S. is on a path to economic Armageddon. Shorn of industry, dependent on offshored manufactured goods and services, and deprived of the dollar as reserve currency, the U.S. will become a Third World country. Gomery notes that it would be very difficult—perhaps impossible—for the U.S. to re-acquire the manufacturing capability that it gave away to other countries.

It is a mystery how a people, whose economic policy is turning them into a Third World country with its university graduates working as waitresses, bartenders, and driving cabs, can regard themselves as a hegemonic power even as they build up war debts that are further undermining their ability to pay their import bills.

SEPTEMBER 20, 2007

CHAPTER 3

Outsourcing the American Economy: A Greater Threat Than Terrorism

I S OFFSHORE OUTSOURCING GOOD OR HARMFUL FOR AMERICA? To convince Americans of outsourcing's benefits, corporate outsourcers sponsor misleading one-sided "studies."

Only a small handful of people have looked objectively at the issue. These few and the large number of Americans whose careers have been destroyed by outsourcing have a different view of outsourcing's impact than the corporate-sponsored studies. But so far there has been no debate, just a shouting down of skeptics as "protectionists."

Now comes an important new book, *Outsourcing America*, published by the American Management Association. The authors, two brothers, Ron and Anil Hira, are experts on the subject. One is a professor at the Rochester Institute of Technology, and the other is a professor at Simon Fraser University.

The authors note that despite the enormity of the stakes for all Americans, a state of denial exists among policymakers, economists and outsourcing's corporate champions about the adverse effects on the U.S. The Hira brothers succeed in their task of interjecting harsh reality where delusion has ruled.

In what might be an underestimate, a University of California study concludes that 14 million white-collar jobs are vulnerable to being outsourced offshore. These are not only call-center operators, customer service and back-office jobs, but also information technology, accounting, architecture, advanced engineering design, news reporting, stock analysis, and medical and legal services. The authors note that these are the jobs of the American Dream, the jobs of upward mobility that generate the bulk of the tax revenues that fund our education, health, infrastructure, and social security systems.

The loss of these jobs "is fool's gold for companies." Corporate America's short-term mentality, stemming from bonuses tied to quarterly results, is causing U.S. companies to lose not only their best employees—their human capital—but also the consumers who buy their products. Employees displaced by foreigners and left unemployed or in lower paid work have a reduced presence in the consumer market. They provide fewer retirement savings for new investment.

No-think economists assume that new, better jobs are on the way for displaced Americans, but no economists can identify these jobs. The authors point out that "the track record for the re-employment of displaced U.S. workers is abysmal: the Department of Labor reports that more than one in three workers who are displaced remain unemployed, and many of those who are lucky enough to find jobs take major pay cuts. Many former manufacturing workers who were displaced a decade ago because of manufacturing that went offshore took training courses and found jobs in the information technology sector. They are now facing the unenviable situation of having their second career disappear overseas."

American economists are so inattentive to outsourcing's perils that they fail to realize that the same incentive that leads to the outsourcing of one tradable good or service holds for all tradable goods and services. In the 21st century the U.S. economy has only been able to create jobs in nontradable domestic services—the hallmark of a Third World labor force.

Prior to the advent of offshore outsourcing, U.S. employees were shielded against low wage foreign labor. Americans worked with more capital and better technology, and their higher productivity protected their higher wages.

Outsourcing forces Americans to "compete head-to-head with foreign workers" by "undermining U.S. workers' primary competitive advantage over foreign workers: their physical presence in the U.S." and "by providing those overseas workers with the same technologies."

The result is a lose-lose situation for American employees, and eventually for American businesses and the American government. Outsourcing has brought about record unemployment in engineering fields and a major drop in university enrollments in technical and scientific disciplines. Even many of the remaining jobs are being filled by lower paid foreigners brought in on H-1B and L-1 visas. American employees are discharged after being forced to train their foreign replacements.

U.S. corporations justify their offshore operations as essential to gain a foothold in emerging Asian markets. The Hira brothers believe this is self-delusion. "There is no evidence that they will be able to out-compete local Chinese and Indian companies, who are very rapidly assimilating the technology and know-how from the local U.S. plants. In fact, studies show that Indian IT companies have been consistently out-competing their U.S. counterparts, even in U.S. markets. Thus, it is time for CEOs to start thinking about whether they are fine with their own jobs being outsourced as well."

The authors note that the national security implications of outsourcing "have been largely ignored."

Outsourcing is rapidly eroding America's superpower status. Beginning in 2002 the U.S. began running trade deficits in advanced technology products with Asia, Mexico, and Ireland. As these countries are not leaders in advanced technology, the deficits obviously stem from U.S. offshore manufacturing. In effect, the U.S. is giving away its technology, which is rapidly being captured, while U.S. firms reduce themselves to a brand name with a sales force.

In an appendix, the authors provide a devastating exposé of the three "studies" that have been used to silence doubts about offshore outsourcing—the Global Insight study (March 2004) for the Information Technology Association of America (ITAA), the Catherine Mann study (December 2003) for the Institute for International Economics, and the McKinsey Global Institute study (August 2003).

The ITAA is a lobbying group for outsourcing. The ITAA spun the results of the study by releasing only the executive summary to reporters who agreed not to seek outside opinion prior to writing their stories.

Mann's study is "an unreasonably optimistic forecast based on faulty logic and a poor understanding of technology and strategy."

The McKinsey report "should be viewed as a self-interested lobbying document that presents an unrealistically optimistic estimate of the impact of offshore outsourcing and an undeveloped and politically unviable solution to the problems they identify."

Outsourcing America is a powerful work. Only fools will continue clinging to the premise that outsourcing is good for America.

APRIL 19, 2005

CHAPTER 4

The New Face of Class War

T HE ATTACKS ON MIDDLE-CLASS JOBS ARE LENDING NEW MEANING to the phrase "class war." The ladders of upward mobility are being dismantled. America, the land of opportunity, is giving way to ever deepening polarization between rich and poor.

The assault on jobs predates the Bush regime. However, the loss of middle-class jobs has become particularly intense in the 21st century, and, like other pressing problems, has been ignored by President Bush, who is focused on waging war in the Middle East and building a police state at home. The lives and careers that are being lost to the carnage of a gratuitous war in Iraq are paralleled by the economic destruction of careers, families, and communities in the U.S.A. Since the days of President Franklin D. Roosevelt in the 1930s, the U.S. government has sought to protect employment of its citizens. Bush has turned his back on this responsibility. He has given his support to the offshoring of American jobs that is eroding the living standards of Americans. It is another example of his betrayal of the public trust.

"Free trade" and "globalization" are the guises behind which class war is being conducted against the middle class by both political parties. Patrick J. Buchanan, a three-time contender for the presidential nomination, put it well when he wrote that NAFTA and the various so-called trade agreements were never trade deals. The agreements were enabling acts that enabled U.S. corporations to dump their American workers, avoid Social Security taxes, health care, and pensions, and move their factories offshore to locations where labor is cheap.

The offshore outsourcing of American jobs has nothing to do with free trade based on comparative advantage. Offshoring is labor arbitrage. First world capital and technology are not seeking comparative advantage at home in order to compete abroad. They are seeking absolute advantage abroad in cheap labor.

Two recent developments made possible the supremacy of absolute over comparative advantage: the high speed Internet and the collapse of world socialism, which opened China's and India's vast under-utilized labor resources to First World capital.

In times past, First World workers had nothing to fear from cheap labor abroad. Americans worked with superior capital, technology, and business organization. This made Americans far more productive than Indians and Chinese, and, as it was not possible for U.S. firms to substitute cheaper foreign labor for U.S. labor, American jobs and living standards were not threatened by low wages abroad or by the products that these low wages produced.

The advent of offshoring has made it possible for U.S. firms using First World capital and technology to produce goods and services for the U.S. market with foreign labor. The result is to separate Americans' incomes from the production of the goods and services that they consume. This new development, often called "globalization," allows cheap foreign labor to work with the same capital, technology, and business know-how as U.S. workers. The foreign workers are now as productive as Americans, with the difference being that the large excess supply of labor that overhangs labor markets in China and India keeps wages in these countries low. Labor that is equally productive but paid a fraction of the wage is a magnet for Western capital and technology.

Although a new development, offshoring is destroying entire industries, occupations and communities in the United States. The devastation of U.S. manufacturing employment was waved away with promises that a "new economy" based on high-tech knowledge jobs would take its place. Education and retraining were touted as the answer.

In testimony before the U.S.-China Commission, I explained that offshoring is the replacement of U.S. labor with foreign labor in U.S. production functions over a wide range of tradable goods and services. (Tradable goods and services are those that can be exported or that are competitive with imports. Nontradable goods and services are those that only have domestic markets and no import competition. For example, barbers and dentists offer nontradable services. Examples of nontradable goods are perishable, locally produced fruits and vegetables and specially fabricated parts of local machine shops.) As the production of most tradable goods and services can be moved offshore, there are no replacement occupations for which to train except in domestic "hands on" services such as barbers, manicurists, and hospital orderlies. No country benefits from trading its professional jobs, such as engineering, for domestic service jobs.

At a Brookings Institution conference in Washington, D.C., in January 2004, I predicted that if the pace of jobs outsourcing and occupational destruction continued, the U.S. would be a Third World country in 20 years. Despite my regular updates on the poor performance of U.S. job growth in the 21st century, economists have insisted that offshoring is a manifestation of free trade and can only have positive benefits overall for Americans.

Reality has contradicted the glib economists. The new high-tech knowledge jobs are being outsourced abroad even faster than the old manufacturing jobs. Establishment economists are beginning to see the light. Writing in *Foreign Affairs* (March/April 2006), Princeton economist and former Federal Reserve vice chairman Alan Blinder concluded that economists who insist that offshore outsourcing is merely a routine extension of international trade are overlooking a major transformation with significant consequences. Blinder estimates that 42–56 million American service sector jobs are susceptible to offshore outsourcing. Whether all these jobs leave, U.S. salaries will be forced down by the willingness of foreigners to do the work for less.

Software engineers and information technology workers have been especially hard hit. Jobs offshoring, which began with call centers and back-office operations, is rapidly moving up the value chain. *Business Week*'s Michael Mandel compared starting salaries in 2005 with those in 2001. He found a 12.7 per cent decline in computer science pay, a 12 per cent decline in computer engineering pay, and a 10.2 per cent decline in electrical engineering pay. Marketing salaries experienced a 6.5 per cent decline, and business administration salaries fell 5.7 per cent. Despite a make-work law for accountants known by the names of its congressional sponsors, Sarbanes-Oxley, even accounting majors were offered 2.3 per cent less.

Using the same sources as the *Business Week* article (salary data from the National Association of Colleges and Employers, and Bureau of Labor Statistics data for inflation adjustment), professor Norm Matloff at the University of California, Davis, made the same comparison for master's degree graduates. He found that between 2001 and 2005 starting pay for master's degrees in computer science, computer engineering, and electrical engineering fell 6.6 per cent, 13.7 per cent, and 9.4 per cent respectively.

On February 22, 2006, CNNMoney.com staff writer Shaheen Pasha reported that America's large financial institutions are moving "large portions of their investment banking operations abroad." Offshoring is now killing American jobs in research and analytic operations, foreign exchange trades, and highly complicated credit derivatives contracts. Deal making responsibility itself may eventually move abroad. Deloitte & Touche says that the financial services industry will move 20 per cent of its total costs base offshore by the end of 2010. As the costs are lower in India, the move will represent more than 20 per cent of the business. A job on Wall Street is a declining option for bright young persons with high stress tolerance as America's last remaining advantage is outsourced.

According to Norm Augustine, former CEO of Lockheed Martin, even McDonald's jobs are on the way offshore. Augustine reports that McDonald's is experimenting with replacing error-prone order takers with a system that transmits orders via satellite to a central location and from there to the person preparing the order. The technology lets the orders be taken in India or China at costs below the U.S. minimum wage and without the liabilities of U.S. employees.

American economists, some from incompetence and some from being bought and paid for, described globalization as a "win-win" development. It was supposed to work like this: The U.S. would lose market share in tradable manufactured goods and make up the job and economic loss with highly-educated workers. The win for America would be lower-priced manufactured goods and a white-collar work force. The win for China would be manufacturing jobs that would bring economic development to that country.

It did not work out this way, as Morgan Stanley's Stephen Roach, formerly a cheerleader for globalization, recently admitted. It has become apparent that job creation and real wages in the developed economies are seriously lagging behind their historical norms as offshore outsourcing displaces the "new economy" jobs in "software programming, engineering, design, and the medical profession, as well as a broad array of professionals in the legal, accounting, actuarial, consulting, and financial services industries." The real state of the U.S. job market is revealed by a *Chicago Sun-Times* report on January 26, 2006, that 25,000 people applied for 325 jobs at a new Chicago Wal-Mart.

According to the BLS payroll jobs data, over the past half-decade (January 2001–January 2006, the data series available at time of writing) the U.S. economy created 1,050,000 net new private sector jobs and 1,009,000 net new government jobs for a total five-year figure of 2,059,000. That is 7 million jobs short of keeping up with population growth, definitely a serious job shortfall.

The BLS payroll jobs data contradict the hype from business organizations, such as the U.S. Chamber of Commerce, that offshore outsourcing is good for America. Large corporations, which have individually dismissed thousands of their U.S. employees and replaced them with foreigners, claim that jobs outsourcing allows them to save money that can be used to hire more Americans. The corporations and the business organizations are very successful in placing this disinformation in the media. The lie is repeated everywhere and has become a mantra among no-think economists and politicians. However, no sign of these jobs can be found in the payroll jobs data. But there is abundant evidence of the lost American jobs.

During the past five years (January 01–January 06), the information sector of the U.S. economy lost 644,000 jobs, or 17.4 per cent of its work force. Computer systems design and related work lost 105,000 jobs, or 8.5 per cent of its work force. Clearly, jobs offshoring is not creating jobs in computers and information technology. Indeed, jobs offshoring is not even creating jobs in related fields.

U.S. manufacturing lost 2.9 million jobs, almost 17 per cent of the manufacturing work force. The wipeout is across the board. Not a single manufacturing payroll classification created a single new job.

The declines in some manufacturing sectors have more in common with a country undergoing saturation bombing during war than with a "super-economy" that is "the envy of the world." In five years, communications equipment lost 42 per cent of its work force. Semiconductors and electronic components lost 37 per cent of its work force. The work force in computers and electronic products declined 30 per cent. Electrical equipment and appliances lost 25 per cent of its employees. The work force in motor vehicles and parts declined 12 per cent. Furniture and related products lost 17 per cent of its jobs. Apparel manufacturers lost almost half of the work force. Employment in textile mills declined 43 per cent. Paper and paper products lost one-fifth of its jobs. The work force in plastics and rubber products declined by 15 per cent.

For the five-year period, U.S. job growth was limited to four areas: education and health services, state and local government, leisure and hospitality, and financial services. There was no U.S. job growth outside these four areas.

Oracle, for example, which has been handing out thousands of pink slips, has recently announced 2,000 more jobs being moved to India. How is Oracle's move of U.S. jobs to India creating American jobs in nontradable services such as waitresses and bartenders, hospital orderlies, state and local government, and credit agencies? Oracle is creating more unemployed Americans to compete for lower paid jobs.

Engineering jobs in general are in decline, because the manufacturing sectors that employ engineers are in decline. During the last five years, the U.S. work force lost 1.2 million jobs in the manufacture of machinery, computers, electronics, semiconductors, communication equipment, electrical equipment, motor vehicles, and transportation equipment. The BLS payroll jobs numbers show a total of 69,000 jobs created in all fields of architecture and engineering, including clerical personnel, over the past five years. That comes to a mere 14,000 jobs per year (including clerical workers). What is the annual graduating class in engineering and architecture? How is there a shortage of engineers when more graduate than can be employed?

Of course, many new graduates take jobs opened by retirements. We would have to know the retirement rates to get a solid handle on the fate of new graduates. But this fate cannot be very pleasant, with declining employment in the manufacturing sectors that employ engineers and a minimum of 65,000 H-1B work visas annually for foreigners plus an indeterminate number of L-1 work visas.

It is not only the Bush regime that bases its policies on lies. Not content with moving Americans' jobs abroad, corporations want to fill the jobs remaining in America with foreigners on work visas. Business organizations allege shortages of engineers, scientists, and even nurses. Business organizations have successfully used pubic relations firms and bought-and-paid-for "economic studies" to convince policymakers that American business cannot function without H-1B visas that permit the importation of indentured employees from abroad who are paid less than the going U.S. salaries. The so-called shortage is, in fact, a replacement of American employees with foreign employees, with the soon-to-be-discharged American employee first required to train his replacement.

It is amazing to see free-market economists rush to the defense of H-1B visas. The visas are nothing but a subsidy to U.S. companies at the expense of U.S. citizens. Keep in mind the H-1B subsidy to U.S. corporations for employing foreign workers in place of Americans as we examine the Labor Department's job projections over the 2004–2014 decade.

All of the occupations with the largest projected employment growth (in terms of the number of jobs) over the next decade are in nontradable domestic services. The top ten sources of the most jobs in "superpower" America are: retail salespersons, registered nurses, postsecondary teachers, customer service representatives, janitors and cleaners, waiters and waitresses, food preparation (includes fast food), home health aides, nursing aides, orderlies and attendants, general and operations managers. Note than none of this projected employment growth will contribute one nickel toward producing goods and services that could be exported to help close the huge U.S. trade deficit. Note, also, that few of these job classifications require a college education.

Among the fastest growing occupations (in terms of rate of growth), seven of the ten are in health care and social assistance. The three remaining fields are: network systems and data analysis with 126,000 jobs projected, or 12,600 per year; computer software engineering applications with 222,000 jobs projected, or 22,200 per year; and computer software engineering systems software with 146,000 jobs projected, or 14,600 per year.

Assuming these projections are realized, how many of the computer engineering and network systems jobs will go to Americans? Not many, considering the 65,000 H-1B visas each year (bills have been introduced in Congress to raise the number) and the loss during the past five years of 761,000 jobs in the information sector and computer systems design and related sectors.

Judging from its ten-year jobs projections, the U.S. Department of Labor does not expect to see any significant high-tech job growth in the U.S. The knowledge jobs are being outsourced even more rapidly than the manufacturing jobs. The so-called "new economy" was just another hoax perpetrated on the American people.

If outsourcing jobs offshore is good for U.S. employment, why won't the U.S. Department of Commerce release the 200-page, $335,000 study of the impact of the offshoring of U.S. high-tech jobs? Republican political appointees reduced the 200-page report to 12 pages of public relations hype and refuse to allow the Department of Commerce's Technology Administration experts who wrote the report to testify before Congress. Democrats on the House Science Committee are unable to pry the study out of the hands of Commerce Secretary Carlos Gutierrez. On March 29, 2006, Republicans on the House Science Committee voted down a resolution designed to force the Commerce Department to release the study to Congress. Obviously, the facts don't fit the Bush regime's globalization hype.

The BLS payroll data that we have been examining tracks employment by industry classification. This is not the same thing as occupational classification. For example, companies in almost every industry and area of business employ people in computer-related occupations. A recent study from the Association for Computing Machinery claims, "Despite all the publicity in the United States about jobs being lost to India and China, the size of the IT employment market in the United States today is higher than it was at the height of the dot.com boom. Information technology appears as though it will be a growth area at least for the coming decade."

We can check this claim by turning to the BLS Occupational Employment Statistics. We will look at "computer and mathematical employment" and "architecture and engineering employment."

Computer and mathematical employment includes such fields as "software engineers applications," "software engineers systems software," "computer programmers," "network systems and data communications," and "mathematicians." Has this occupation been a source of job growth? In November of 2000 this occupation employed 2,932,810 people. In November of 2004 (the latest data available), this occupation employed 2,932,790, or 20 people fewer. Employment in this field has been stagnant for four years.

During these four years, there have been employment shifts within the various fields of this occupation. For example, employment of computer programmers declined by 134,630, while employment of software engineers applications rose by 65,080, and employment of software engineers systems software rose by 59,600. (These shifts probably merely reflect change in job title from programmer to software engineer.)

These figures do not tell us whether any gain in software engineering jobs went to Americans. According to professor Norm Matloff, in 2002 there were 463,000 computer-related H-1B visa holders in the U.S. Similarly, the 134,630 lost computer programming jobs (if not merely a job title change) may have been outsourced offshore to foreign affiliates.

Architecture and engineering employment includes all the architecture and engineering fields except software engineering. The total employment of architects and engineers in the U.S. declined by 120,700 between November 1999 and November 2004. Employment declined by 189,940 between November 2000 and November 2004, and by 103,390 between November 2001 and November 2004.

There are variations among fields. Between November 2000 and November 2004, for example, U.S. employment of electrical engineers fell by 15,280. Employment of computer hardware engineers rose by 15,990 (possibly these are job title reclassifications). Overall, however, over 100,000 engineering jobs were lost. We do not know how many of the lost jobs were outsourced offshore to foreign affiliates or how many American engineers were dismissed and replaced by foreign holders of H-1B or L-1 visas.

Clearly, engineering and computer-related employment in the U.S.A. has not been growing, whether measured by industry or by occupation. Moreover, with a half million or more foreigners in the U.S. on work visas, the overall employment numbers do not represent employment of Americans.

American employees have been abandoned by American corporations and by their representatives in Congress. America remains a land of opportunity—but for foreigners—not for the native born. A country whose work force is concentrated in domestic nontradable services has no need for scientists and engineers and no need for universities. Even the projected jobs in nursing and school teaching can be filled by foreigners on H-1B visas.

The myth has been firmly established that the jobs the U.S. is outsourcing offshore are being replaced with better jobs. There is no sign of these jobs in the payroll jobs data or in the occupational employment statistics. When a country loses entry-level jobs, it has no one to promote to senior level jobs. When manufacturing leaves, so does engineering, design, research and development, and innovation itself.

On February 16, 2006, the *New York Times* reported on a new study presented to the National Academies of Science that concludes that outsourcing is climbing the skills ladder. A survey of 200 multinational corporations representing 15 industries in the U.S. and Europe found that 38 per cent planned to change substantially the worldwide distribution of their research and development work, sending it to India and China. According to the *New York Times*, "More companies in the survey said they planned to decrease research and development employment in the United States and Europe than planned to increase employment."

The study and the discussion it provoked came to untenable remedies. Many believe that a primary reason for the shift of R&D to India and China is the erosion of scientific prowess in the U.S. due to lack of math and science proficiency of American students and their reluctance to pursue careers in science and engineering. This belief begs the question why students would chase after careers that are being outsourced abroad.

The main author of the study, Georgia Tech professor Marie Thursby, believes that American science and engineering depend on having "an environment that fosters the development of a high-quality work force and productive collaboration between corporations and universities." The dean of Engineering at the University of California, Berkeley, thinks the answer is to recruit the top people in China and India and bring them to Berkeley. No one seems to understand that research, development, design, and innovation take place in countries where things are made. The loss of manufacturing means ultimately the loss of engineering and science. The newest plants embody the latest technology. If these plants are abroad, that is where the cutting edge resides.

The denial of jobs reality has become an art form for economists, libertarians, the Bush regime, and journalists. Except for CNN's Lou Dobbs, no accurate reporting is available in the "mainstream media."

Economists have failed to examine the incompatibility of offshoring with free trade. Economists are so accustomed to shouting down protectionists that they dismiss any complaint about globalization's impact on domestic jobs as the ignorant voice of a protectionist seeking to preserve the buggy whip industry. Matthew J. Slaughter, a Dartmouth economics professor rewarded for his service to offshoring with appointment to President Bush's Council of Economic Advisers, suffered no harm to his reputation when he carelessly wrote, "For every one job that U.S. multinationals created abroad in their foreign affiliates, they created nearly two U.S. jobs in their parent operations." In other words, Slaughter claims that offshoring is creating more American jobs than foreign ones.

How did Slaughter arrive at this conclusion? Not by consulting the BLS payroll jobs data or the BLS Occupational Employment Statistics. Instead, Slaughter measured the growth of U.S. multinational employment and failed to take into account the two reasons for the increase in multinational employment: (1) Multinationals acquired many existing smaller firms, thus raising multinational employment but not overall employment, and (2) many U.S. firms established foreign operations for the first time and thereby became multinationals, thus adding their existing employment to Slaughter's number for multinational employment.

ABC News' John Stossel, a libertarian hero, recently made a similar error. In debunking Lou Dobbs' concern with U.S. jobs lost to offshore outsourcing, Stossel invoked the California-based company, Collabnet. He quotes the CEO's claim that outsourcing saves his company money and lets him hire more Americans. Turning to Collabnet's webpage, it is very instructive to see the employment opportunities that the company posts for the United States and for India.

In India, Collabnet has openings (at time of writing) for eight engineers, a sales engineer, a technical writer, and a telemarketing representative. In the U.S. Collabnet has openings for one engineer, a receptionist/office assistant, and positions in marketing, sales, services, and operations. Collabnet is a perfect example of what Lou Dobbs and I report: the engineering and design jobs move abroad, and Americans are employed to sell and market the foreign-made products.

Other forms of deception are widely practiced. For example, Matthew Spiegleman, a Conference Board economist, claims that manufacturing jobs are only slightly higher paid than domestic service jobs, so there is no meaningful loss in income to Americans from offshoring. He reaches this conclusion by comparing only hourly pay and leaving out the longer manufacturing workweek and the associated benefits, such as health care and pensions.

Occasionally, however, real information escapes the spin machine. In February 2006 the National Association of Manufacturers, one of offshoring's greatest boosters, released a report, "U.S. Manufacturing Innovation at Risk," by economists Joel Popkin and Kathryn Kobe. The economists find that U.S. industry's investment in research and development is not languishing after all. It just appears to be languishing, because it is rapidly being shifted overseas: "Funds provided for foreign-performed R&D have grown by almost 73 per cent between 1999 and

2003, with a 36 per cent increase in the number of firms funding foreign R&D."

U.S. industry is still investing in R&D after all; it is just not hiring Americans to do the research and development. U.S. manufacturers still make things, only less and less in America with American labor. U.S. manufacturers still hire engineers, only they are foreign ones, not American ones.

In other words, everything is fine for U.S. manufacturers. It is just their former American work force that is in the doldrums. As these Americans happen to be customers for U.S. manufacturers, U.S. brand names will gradually lose their U.S. market. U.S. household median income has fallen for the past five years. Consumer demand has been kept alive by consumers' spending their savings and home equity and going deeper into debt. It is not possible for debt to forever rise faster than income.

The United States is the first country in history to destroy the prospects and living standards of its labor force. It is amazing to watch freedom-loving libertarians and free-market economists serve as apologists for the dismantling of the ladders of upward mobility that made the America of old an opportunity society.

America is seeing a widening polarization into rich and poor. The resulting political instability and social strife will be terrible.

SEPTEMBER 30, 2006

CHAPTER 5

Empire on the Brink:
Zealots Bring Disaster to America

MARCH 12, 2008. CRUDE OIL FOR APRIL DELIVERY HIT $110 PER barrel. The U.S. dollar fell to a new low against the euro. It now takes $1.55 to purchase one euro.

These new highs against the dollar are the ongoing story of the collapse of the U.S. dollar as world reserve currency and corresponding collapse of American power.

Each new decision from the insane Bush regime pushes the dollar a little further along to oblivion. The same Fed announcement that boosted the stock market on March 11 sent the dollar reeling and the price of oil up. The Fed's announcement that it and other central banks are going to deal with the derivative crisis by monetizing $200 billion of the troubled instruments signaled more dollar inflation.

Of course, something needed to be done to forestall an implosion of the financial system, but a less costly alternative was at hand. The mark-to-market rule could have been suspended in order to halt the forced sale and write down of assets and to provide time in which to sort out derivative values, which are higher than the fire sale prices.

More pressure on the dollar resulted from the decision to award the European company, Airbus, a $40 billion contract that could reach $100 billion to build U.S. Air Force tankers. In simple terms, that means another $40 to $100 billion added to the U.S. trade deficit, and a loss of $40 to $100 billion in U.S. Gross Domestic Product and associated jobs.

Of course, the Bush regime had to award the contract to Europe as a payoff for Europe's support of the Bush regime's wars of aggression in the Middle East. Europe is not going to provide Bush with diplomatic cover for his wars and NATO troops for his war in Afghanistan without a payoff.

Here is the picture: The U.S. economy, which has been kept alive by enormous debt expansion that has over-reached its limit, is falling into recession. The traditional way out by expanding the supply of money and credit is blocked by the impaired banking system, the levels of consumer debt, and the collapsing value of the U.S. dollar.

The Bush regime is attempting to bypass the stalled credit expansion by sending Americans $600 checks, money that will mainly be used to reduce existing credit card debt and not to fund new consumption.

The U.S. is dependent on foreigners not only for energy but also for manufactured goods and advanced technology products. The U.S. is dependent on foreigners to finance our consumption of $800 billion annually more than the U.S. produces. The U.S. is dependent on foreigners to finance its red ink wars, and the U.S. government's budget deficit is now expanding as tax revenues decline with the declining economy.

The bottom line: U.S. power is enfeebled. U.S. power depends on the willingness of foreigners to finance our wars and on the willingness of foreigners to continue to accumulate depreciating dollar assets. The U.S. cannot close its trade deficit. Oil prices are rising, and offshore production of goods and services for U.S. markets results in a dollar-for-dollar increase in imports, while reducing the supply of domestic goods available for export.

The U.S. cannot close its budget deficit while it is squandering vast sums on wars that serve no U.S. purpose, handing out $150 billion in red ink rebates, and falling into recession.

U.S. living standards, which have been stagnant for years, will plummet once dollar decline forces China off the dollar peg. So far prices of the Chinese-made goods on Wal-Mart shelves have not risen, because the Chinese currency, pegged to the dollar, falls in value with the dollar. In a word, tottering U.S. living standards are being supported by China's willingness to subsidize U.S. consumption by keeping its currency undervalued.

The U.S. is overextended economically and militarily, just as was Great Britain with the fall of France in the opening days of World War II. The British had the Americans to bail them out. After the chewing gum and bailing wire patch-ups are exhausted, who is going to bail us out?

MARCH 13, 2008

CHAPTER 6

The Bitter Fruits of Deregulation

R EMEMBER THE GOOD OLD DAYS WHEN THE ECONOMIC THREAT was mere recession? The Federal Reserve would encourage the economy with low interest rates until the economy overheated. Prices would rise, and unions would strike for higher benefits. Then the Fed would put on the brakes by raising interest rates. Money supply growth would fall. Inventories would grow, and layoffs would result. When the economy cooled down, the cycle would start over.

The nice thing about 20th century recessions was that the jobs returned when the Federal Reserve lowered interest rates and consumer demand increased. In the 21st century, the jobs that have been moved offshore do not come back. More than 3 million U.S. manufacturing jobs have been lost while Bush was in the White House. Those jobs represent consumer income and career opportunities that America will never see again.

In the 21st century the U.S. economy has produced net new jobs only in low paid domestic services, such as waitresses, bartenders, hospital orderlies, and retail clerks. The kind of jobs that provided ladders of upward mobility into the middle class are being exported abroad or filled by foreigners brought in on work visas. Today when you purchase an American name brand, you are supporting economic growth and consumer incomes in China and Indonesia, not in Detroit and Cincinnati.

In the 20th century, economic growth resulted from improved technologies, new investment, and increases in labor productivity, which raised consumers' incomes and purchasing power. In contrast, in the 21st century, economic growth has resulted from debt expansion.

Most Americans have experienced little, if any, income growth in the 21st century. Instead, consumers have kept the economy going by maxing out their credit cards and refinancing their mortgages in order to consume the equity in their homes.

The income gains of the 21st century have gone to corporate chief executives, shareholders of offshoring corporations, and financial corporations.

By replacing $20 an hour U.S. labor with $1 an hour Chinese labor, the profits of U.S. offshoring corporations have boomed, thus driving up share prices and "performance" bonuses for corporate CEOs. With Bush/Cheney, the Republicans have resurrected their policy of favoring the rich over the poor. John McCain captured today's high income class with his quip that you are middle class if you have an annual income less than $5 million.

Financial companies have made enormous profits by securitizing income flows from unknown risks and selling asset-backed securities to pension funds and investors at home and abroad.

Today recession is only a small part of the threat that we face. Financial deregulation, Alan Greenspan's low interest rates, and the belief that the market is the best regulator of risks, have created a highly leveraged pyramid of risk without adequate capital or collateral to back the risk. Consequently, a wide variety of financial institutions are threatened with insolvency, threatening a collapse comparable to the bank failures that shrank the supply of money and credit and produced the Great Depression.

Washington has been slow to recognize the current problem. A millstone around the neck of every financial institution is the mark-to-market rule, an ill-advised "reform" from a previous crisis that was blamed on fraudulent accounting that over-valued assets on the books. As a result, today institutions have to value their assets at current market value.

In the current crisis the rule has turned out to be a curse. Asset-backed securities, such as collateralized mortgage obligations, faced their first market pricing in panicked circumstances. The owner of a bond backed by 1,000 mortgages doesn't know how many of the mortgages are good and how many are bad. The uncertainty erodes the value of the bond.

If significant amounts of such untested securities are on the balance sheet, insolvency rears its ugly head. The bonds get dumped in order to realize some part of their value. Merrill Lynch sold its asset-backed securities for twenty cents on the dollar, although it is unlikely that 80 per cent of the instruments were worthless.

The mark-to-market rule, together with the suspect values of the asset backed securities and collateral debt obligations and swaps, allowed short sellers to make fortunes by driving down the share prices of the investment banks, thus worsening the crisis. With their capitalization shrinking, the investment banks could no longer borrow. The authorities took their time in halting short-selling, and short-selling is set to resume soon.

If the mark-to-market rule had been suspended and short-selling prohibited, the crisis would have been mitigated. Instead, the crisis intensified, provoking the U.S. Treasury to propose to take responsibility for $700 billion more in troubled financial instruments in addition to the Fannie Mae, Freddie Mac, and AIG bailouts. Treasury guarantees are also being extended to money market funds.

All of this makes sense at a certain level. But what if the $700 billion doesn't stem the tide and another $700 billion is needed? At what point does the Treasury's assumption of liabilities erode its own credit standing?

This crisis comes at the worst possible time. Gratuitous wars and military spending in pursuit of U.S. world hegemony have inflated the federal budget deficit, which recession is further enlarging. Massive trade deficits, magnified by the offshoring of goods and services, cannot be eliminated by U.S. export capability.

These large deficits are financed by foreigners, and foreign unease has resulted in a decline in the U.S. dollar's value compared to other tradable currencies, precious metals, and oil.

The U.S. Treasury does not have $700 billion on hand with which to buy the troubled assets from the troubled institutions. The Treasury will have to borrow the $700 billion from abroad.

The dependency of Treasury Secretary Henry Paulson's bailout scheme on foreign willingness to absorb more Treasury paper in order that the Treasury has the money to bail out the troubled institutions is heavy proof that the U.S. is in a financially dependent position that is inconsistent with that of America's "superpower" status.

The U.S. is not a superpower. The U.S. is a financially dependent country that foreign lenders can close down at will.

Washington still hasn't learned this. American hubris can lead the administration and Congress into a bailout solution that the rest of the world, which has to finance it, might not accept.

Currently, the fight between the administration and Congress over the bailout is whether the bailout will include the Democrats' poor constituencies as well as the Republicans' rich ones. The Republicans, for the most part, and their media shills are doing their best to exclude the ordinary American from the rescue plan.

A less appreciated feature of Paulson's bailout plan is his demand for freedom from accountability. Congress balked at Paulson's demand that the executive branch's conduct of the bailout be non-reviewable by Congress or the courts: "Decisions by the Secretary pursuant to the authority of this Act are non-reviewable and committed to agency discretion." However, Congress substituted for its own authority a "board" that possibly will consist of the bailed-out parties, by which I mean Republican and Democratic constituencies. The control over the financial system that the bailout would give to the executive branch could mean, in effect, state capitalism or fascism.

If we add state capitalism to the Bush administration's success in eroding both the U.S. Constitution and the power of Congress, we may be witnessing the death of accountable constitutional government.

The U.S. might also be on the verge of a decision by foreign lenders to cease financing a country that claims to be a hegemonic power with the right and the virtue to impose its will on the rest of the world. The U.S. is able to be at war in Iraq and Afghanistan and is able to pick fights with Iran, Pakistan, and Russia, because the Chinese, the Japanese and the sovereign wealth funds of the oil kingdoms finance America's wars and military budgets. Aside from nuclear weapons, which are also in the hands of other countries, the U.S. has no assets of its own with which to pursue its control over the world.

The U.S. cannot be a hegemonic power without foreign financing. All indications are that the rest of the world is tiring of U.S. arrogance.

If the U.S. Treasury's assumption of bailout responsibilities becomes excessive, the U.S. dollar will lose its reserve currency role. The minute that occurs, foreign financing of America's twin deficits will cease, as will the bailout. The U.S. government would have to turn to the printing of paper money.

For now this pending problem is hidden from view, because in times of panic, the tradition is to flee into "safety," that is, into U.S. Treasury debt obligations. The safety of Treasuries will be revealed by the extent of the bailout.

SEPTEMBER 24, 2008

CHAPTER 7

Economic Treason

THE JUNE 2005 PAYROLL JOBS REPORT DID NOT RECEIVE MUCH attention due to the July 4 holiday, but the depressing 21st century job performance of the U.S. economy continues unabated.

- Only 144,000 private sector jobs were created, each one of which was in domestic services.

- 56,000 jobs were created in professional and business services, about half of which are in administrative and waste services.

- 38,000 jobs were created in education and health services, almost all of which are in health care and social assistance.

- 19,000 jobs were created in leisure and hospitality, almost all of which are waitresses and bartenders.

- Membership associations and organizations created 10,000 jobs and repair and maintenance created 4,000 jobs.

- Financial activities created 16,000 jobs.

This most certainly is not the labor market profile of a First World country, much less a superpower.

Where are the jobs for this year's crop of engineering and science graduates?

U.S. manufacturing lost another 24,000 jobs in June.

A country that doesn't manufacture doesn't need many engineers. And the few engineering jobs available go to foreigners.

Readers have sent me employment listings from U.S. software development firms. The listings are discriminatory against American citizens. One ad from a company in New Jersey that is a developer for many companies, including Oracle, specifies that the applicant must have a TN visa.

A TN or Trade NAFTA visa is what is given to Mexicans and Canadians who are willing to work in the U.S. at below prevailing wages.

Another ad from a software consulting company based in Omaha, Nebraska specifies it wants software engineers who are H-1B transferees. What this means is that the firm is advertising for foreigners already in the U.S. who have H-1B work visas.

The reason the U.S. firms specify that they have employment opportunities only for foreigners who hold work visas is because the foreigners will work for less than the prevailing U.S. salary.

Gentle reader, when you read allegations that there is a shortage of engineers in America, necessitating the importation of foreigners to do the work, you are reading a bald-faced lie. If there were a shortage of American engineers, employers would not word their job listings to read that no American need apply and that they are offering jobs only to foreigners holding work visas.

What kind of country gives preference to foreigners over its own engineering graduates?

What kind of country destroys the job market for its own citizens?

How much longer will parents shell out $100,000 for a college education for a son or daughter who ends up employed as a bartender, waitress, or temp?

JULY 16, 2005

CHAPTER 8

How Inflation Works
(or Why I Can't Buy an Old Ferrari)

ANYONE WHO HAS BEEN ALIVE VERY LONG IS AWARE THAT THE U.S. government has failed on the inflation front. Soft drink machines that once delivered a bottled drink for a nickel now charge a dollar, a 20-fold increase in price.

Until the Reagan administration indexed the income tax, inflation was a boon to government, because by pushing up wages and salaries inflation pushed taxpayers into higher brackets. This allowed the real tax burden on labor to rise without politicians having to raise the tax rates. Inflation also destroyed the value of depreciation allowances, thus raising the tax rate on capital as well.

It is not easy to make the young aware of the long-term rise in prices. The inflation indices are periodically re-based, resulting in measures over time with different years as the base. The Clinton administration further destroyed comparability by substituting a variable basket of goods for the fixed assortment that had previously prevailed. With the Boskin Commission "reform" adopted by the Clinton administration, the Consumer Price Index (CPI) no longer compares apples to apples. If the price of apples rises, the CPI assumes that consumers switch to a cheaper substitute. The "substitution effect" thus underestimates the rate of inflation and destroys the comparability of the inflation rate from one period to the next.

Inflation is inherent in a fractional reserve banking system based on fiat money. Fiat money is not subject to limits on its supply, and fractional reserve banking permits the banking system to create money by expanding loans.

Aware of the ever present threat of inflation from such a system, Milton Friedman advocated a monetary rule that would limit the growth of the money supply to the long-term growth rate of the economy. For example, if the money supply grew 2 to 3 per cent annually in keeping with the increase in real output, prices would remain stable. Perhaps it wasn't a perfect solution, but at least Friedman thought about the problem.

In the post-WW II period, the U.S. has experienced dramatic increases in the growth of money and credit. One way to demonstrate the erosion of the purchasing power of money is to look at the change in the behavior of the prices of used Ferraris. In the 1950s, 1960s, and even the 1970s, Ferrari depreciated rapidly. Well-to-do playboys attracted by the unique cars wanted the latest model, and few other people wanted the maintenance expense associated with the high-performance machines. It was not out of the question for a person with an ordinary income to become the second owner of a Ferrari.

Excepting a few models of high volume and undistinguished performance, today it is totally out of the question that a person lacking an out-sized income or a large inheritance could acquire a previously owned Ferrari.

For example, in 1973 when I left Stanford University I had an opportunity to purchase a 1967 Ferrari 330 GTS. It was a low mileage car in new condition. The asking price was $10,000 and could have been negotiated down. Unfortunately, the Scottish part of my ancestry prevailed, and I did not purchase the Ferrari. Recently at the Monterey auction a 330 GTS sold for $671,000, 67 times its 1973 used car price.

As an assistant professor of economics in 1967, I cut a road test out of *Road & Track* magazine and filed it. The test was one of a 1967 Ferrari 275 GTB/4. The new price was $14,500. I intended to find one in a few years at a substantially depreciated price. At a recent Monetary auction, a 1967 GTB/4 sold for $1,925,000.

What has happened to money that causes a 41-year-old used car to sell for 133 times its new car price?

The abundance of money from a fiat money/fractional reserve banking system raises the price of scarce items that are beautiful and unique, such as Ferraris and antiques. Few Ferrari models were produced in numbers greater than several hundred cars. Perhaps the most famous Ferrari is the 250 GTO. Less than 40 were produced. The GTO, which is street legal, dominated racing and won the World Manufacturers

Championship in 1962, 1963, and 1964. The new car price was $18,000. In 1989 one sold for $13 million. This year one sold for $28 million. I have a friend who bought a used GTO in Europe in the mid-1960s for $9,000 and sold it six months later for the same price.

Ferraris became collectibles, a store of value, a role that the dollar no longer performs. Today collectible cars have become items for speculation. They are flipped in auctions with bids rising several hundred thousand dollars from auction to auction, just as real estate speculators bid up waterfront condo prices and hedge funds bid up oil futures contracts.

The cars are worth so much now that you will never see one on the road, not even in the playgrounds of the rich and famous. The more than 1,500-fold rise in the price of the GTO over the last 45 years makes gold's 28-fold price rise seem insignificant. But both prices show the ruin inflicted on the dollar by our fiat money/fractional reserve system.

OCTOBER 21, 2008

CHAPTER 9

When Greed is Rewarded:
Government of Thieves

J ust as the Bush regime's wars have been used to pour billions of dollars into the pockets of its military-security donor base, the Paulson bailout looks like a Bush regime scheme to incur $700 billion in new public debt in order to transfer the money into the coffers of its financial donor base. The U.S. taxpayers will be left with the interest payments in perpetuity (or inflation if the Fed monetizes the debt), and the number of Wall Street billionaires will grow. As for the U.S. and European governments' purchases of bank shares, that is just a cover for funneling public money into private hands.

The explanations that have been given for the crisis and its bailout are opaque. The U.S. Treasury estimates that as few as 7 per cent of the mortgages are bad. Why then do the U.S., U.K., Germany, and France need to pour more than $2.1 trillion of public money into private financial institutions?

If, as the government tells us, the crisis stems from subprime mortgage defaults reducing the interest payments to the holders of mortgage backed securities, thus driving down their values and threatening the solvency of the institutions that hold them, why isn't the bailout money used to address the problem at its source? If the bailout money was used to refinance troubled mortgages and to pay off foreclosed mortgages, the mortgage-backed securities would be made whole, and it would be unnecessary to pour huge sums of public money into banks. Instead, the bailout money is being used to inject capital into financial institutions and to purchase from them troubled financial instruments.

It is a strange solution that does not address the problem. As the U.S. economy sinks deeper into recession, the mortgage defaults will rise. Thus, the problem will intensify, necessitating the purchase of yet more troubled instruments.

If credit card debt has also been securitized and sold as investments, as the economy worsens defaults on credit card debt will be a replay of the mortgage defaults. How much debt can the Treasury bail out before its own credit rating sinks?

The contribution of credit default swaps to the financial crisis has not been made clear. These swaps are bets that a designated financial instrument will fail. In exchange for "premium" payments, the seller of a swap protects the buyer of the swap from default by, for example, a company's bond that the swap buyer might not even own. If these swaps are also securitized and sold as investments, more nebulous assets appear on balance sheets.

Normally, if you and I make a bet, and I welsh on the bet, it doesn't threaten your solvency. If we place bets with a bookie and the odds go against the bookie, the bookie will fail, as apparently happened to AIG, necessitating a $185 billion bailout of the insurance company, and to Bear Stearns resulting in the demise of the investment bank.

Credit default swaps are a form of unregulated insurance. One danger of the swaps is that they allow speculators to purchase protection against a company defaulting on its bonds, without the speculators having to own the company's bonds. Speculators can then short the company's stock, driving down its price and raising questions about the viability of the company's bonds. This raises the value of the speculators' swaps which can be sold to holders of the company's bonds. By ruining a company's prospects, the speculators make money.

Another danger is that swaps encourage investors to purchase riskier, higher-yielding instruments in the belief that the instruments are insured, but the sellers of swaps have not reserved against them.

Double-counting of assets is also possible if a bank purchases a company's bonds, for example, then purchases credit default swaps on the bonds, and lists both as assets on its balance sheet.

The $185 billion Treasury bailout of AIG is small compared to the $700 billion for the banks, and the emphasis has been on banks, not insurance companies. According to news reports, the sums associated with credit default swaps are far larger than the subprime mortgage derivatives. Have the swaps yet to become major players in the crisis?

The behavior of the stock market does not necessarily tell us anything about the bailout. The financial crisis disrupted lending and thus comprised a threat to non-financial firms. This threat would reflect in the stock market. However, the stock market is also predicting a recession and declining earnings. Thus, people sell stocks hoping to get out before share prices adjust to the new lower earnings.

The bailout package is a result of panic and threats, not of analysis and understanding. Neither Congress nor the public knows the full story. If the problem is the mortgages, why does the bailout leave the mortgages unaddressed and focus instead on pouring vast amounts of public money into private financial institutions?

The purpose of regulation is to restrain greed and to prevent leveraged speculation from threatening the wider society. Congress needs to restore financial regulation, not reward those who caused the crisis.

OCTOBER 17, 2008

CHAPTER 10

A Nation of Waitresses and Bartenders

THE BUREAU OF LABOR STATISTICS PAYROLL JOBS REPORT RELEASED May 5, 2006, says the economy created 131,000 private sector jobs in April. Construction added 10,000 jobs, natural resources, mining and logging added 8,000 jobs, and manufacturing added 19,000. Despite this unusual gain, the economy has 10,000 fewer manufacturing jobs than a year ago.

Most of the April job gain—72 per cent—is in domestic services, with education and health services (primarily health care and social assistance) and waitresses and bartenders accounting for 55,000 jobs or 42 per cent of the total job gain. Financial activities added 26,000 jobs and professional and business services added 28,000. Retail trade lost 36,000 jobs.

During 2001 and 2002 the U.S. economy lost 2,298,000 jobs. These lost jobs were not regained until early in February 2005. From February 2005 through April 2006, the economy has gained 2,584 jobs (mainly in domestic services).

The total job gain for the 64 month period from January 2001 through April 2006 is 7,000,000 jobs less than the 9,600,000 jobs necessary to stay even with population growth during that period. The unemployment rate is low because millions of discouraged workers have dropped out of the work force and are not counted as unemployed.

In 2005 the U.S. had a current account deficit in excess of $800 billion. That means Americans consumed $800 billion more goods and services than they produced. A significant per centage of this figure is offshore production by U.S. companies for American markets.

The U.S. current account deficit as a per cent of Gross Domestic Product is unprecedented. As more jobs and manufacturing are moved offshore, Americans become more dependent on foreign made goods.

The U.S. pays its current account deficit by giving up ownership of its existing assets or wealth. Foreigners don't simply hold the $800 billion in cash. They use it to acquire U.S. equities, real estate, bonds, and entire companies.

The federal budget is also in the red to the tune of about $400 billion. As Americans have ceased to save, the federal government is dependent on foreigners to lend it the money to operate and to wage war in the Middle East.

American consumers are heavily indebted. The growth of consumer debt is what has been fueling the economy. Social Security and Medicare are in financial trouble, as are many company pension plans. Decide for yourself—is this the economic picture of a superpower that can dictate to the world, or is it the picture of a second-rate country dependent on foreigners to finance its consumption and the operation of its government?

No-think economists make rhetorical arguments that the decline of U.S. manufacturing employment reflects higher productivity from technological improvements and not a decline in U.S. manufacturing per se. George Mason University economist Walter Williams recently ridiculed the claim that U.S. manufacturing jobs are moving to China. Williams asks how the U.S. could be losing manufacturing jobs to China when the Chinese are losing jobs faster than the U.S.: "Since 2000, China has lost 4.5 million manufacturing jobs, compared with the loss of 3.1 million in the U.S."

The 4.5 million figure comes from a Conference Board report that is misleading. The report that counts was written by Judith Banister under contract to the U.S. Department of Labor, Bureau of Labor Statistics, and published in November 2005 (www.bls.gov/fls/chinareport.pdf). Banister's report was peer reviewed both within the BLS and externally by persons with expert knowledge of China.

Chinese manufacturing employment has been growing strongly since the 1980s except for a short period in the late 1990s when layoffs resulted from the restructuring and privatization of inefficient state-owned and collectively-owned factories. To equate temporary layoffs from a massive restructuring within manufacturing with U.S. long-term manufacturing job loss indicates carelessness or incompetence.

Banister concludes: "In recent decades, China has become a manufacturing powerhouse. The country's official data showed 83 million manufacturing employees in 2002, but that figure is likely to be understated; the actual number was probably closer to 109 million. By contrast, in 2002, the Group of Seven (G7) major industrialized countries had a total of 53 million manufacturing workers."

The G7 is the U.S. and Europe. In contrast to China's 109,000,000 manufacturing workers, the U.S. has 14,000,000.

When I was Assistant Secretary of the Treasury in the Reagan administration, the U.S. did not have a trade deficit in manufactured goods. Today the U.S. has a $500 billion annual deficit in manufactured goods. If the U.S. is doing as well in manufacturing as no-think economists claim, where did an annual trade deficit in manufactured goods of one-half trillion dollars come from?

If the U.S. is the high-tech leader of the world, why does the U.S. have a trade deficit in advanced technology products with China?

There was a time when American economists were empirical and paid attention to facts. Today American economists are merely the hand-maidens of offshore producers. Apparently, they follow President Bush's lead and do not read newspapers—thus, their ignorance of countless stories of U.S. manufacturers moving entire plants and many thousands of U.S. engineering jobs to China.

Chinese firms, including state-owned firms, have numerous reasons, tax and otherwise, to understate their employment. Banister's report gives the details.

Banister points out that the excess supply of labor in China is about five to six times the size of the total U.S. work force. As a result, there is no shortage of workers in China, nor will there be in the foreseeable future.

The huge excess supply of labor means extremely low Chinese wages. The average Chinese wage is $0.57 per hour, a mere 3 per cent of the average U.S. manufacturing worker's wage. With First World technology, capital, and business know-how crowding into China, virtually free Chinese labor is as productive as U.S. labor. This should make it obvious to anyone who claims to be an economist that offshore production of goods and services is an example of capital seeking absolute advantage in lowest factor cost, not a case of free trade based on comparative advantage.

American economists have failed their country as badly as have the Republican and Democratic parties. The sad fact is that there is no leader in sight capable of reversing the rapid decline of the United States of America.

MAY 8, 2006

CHAPTER 11

Their Own Economic Reality (Or Why Even Jobs at McDonald's Aren't Safe)

WHO CAN FORGET THE NEOCONS' CLAIM THAT UNDER their leadership America creates its own reality? Remember the neocons' Iraq reality—a "cakewalk" war? After years of combat, thousands of casualties, and cost estimated at over $1 trillion, real reality must still compete with the White House spin machine.

One might think that the Iraq experience would restore sober judgment to policymakers. Alas, neocon "reality" has spread everywhere. It has infected the media and the new Federal Reserve Chairman, Ben Bernanke, who just gave Congress an upbeat report on the economy. The robust economy, he declared, could soon lead to inflation and higher interest rates.

Consumers deeper in debt and fresh from their first negative savings rate since the Great Depression show high consumer confidence. It is as if the entire country is on an acid trip or a cocaine trip or whatever it is that lets people create realities for themselves that bear no relation to real reality.

How can the upbeat views be reconciled with the Bureau of Labor Statistics' payroll jobs data, the extraordinary red ink, and exploding trade deficit? Perhaps the answer is that every economic development, no matter how detrimental, is spun as if it were good news. For example, the worsening U.S. trade deficit is spun as evidence of the fast growth of the U.S. economy: the economy is growing so fast it can't meet its needs and must rely on imports. Declining household income is spun as an inflation fighter that keeps mortgage interest rates low. Federal budget deficits are spun as letting taxpayers keep and spend more of their own money. Massive layoffs are spun as evidence that change is so rapid that the work force must constantly upgrade skills and re-educate itself.

The denial of economic reality has become an art form. Accurate economic reporting is not available in the "mainstream media."

Occasionally, real information escapes the spin machine. The National Association of Manufacturers, one of outsourcing's greatest boosters, has just released a report, "U.S. Manufacturing Innovation at Risk," by economists Joel Popkin and Kathryn Kobe. The economists find that U.S. industry's investment in research and development is rapidly being shifted overseas: "Funds provided for foreign-performed R&D have grown by almost 73 per cent between 1999 and 2003, with a 36 per cent increase in the number of firms funding foreign R&D."

U.S. industry is investing in R&D but is not hiring Americans to do the R&D. U.S. manufacturers still make things, only less and less in America with American labor. U.S. manufacturers still hire engineers, only they are foreign ones, not American ones.

It should be obvious to policymakers that relocating the cutting edge of the economy abroad penalizes the U.S. economy and work force and benefits foreign ones. When manufacturing moves abroad, engineering follows. R&D follows engineering, and innovation follows R&D. The entire economy drains away. This is why the "new economy" has not materialized to take the place of the lost "old economy."

The latest technologies go into the newest plants, and those plants are abroad. Innovations take place in new plants as new processes are developed to optimize the efficiency of the new technologies. The skills required to operate new processes call forth investment in education and training. As U.S. manufacturing and R&D move abroad, Indian and Chinese engineering enrollments rise, and U.S. enrollments decline.

The process is a unified whole. It is not possible for a country to lose parts of the process and hold on to other parts. That is why the "new economy" was a hoax from the beginning. As Popkin and Kobe note, new technologies, new manufacturing processes, and new designs take place where things are made. The notion that the U.S. can lose everything else but hold on to innovation is absurd.

Someone needs to tell Congress before they waste yet more borrowed money. In an adjoining column to the N.A.M. report on innovation, the February 6, 2006, *Manufacturing & Technology News* reports that "the U.S. Senate is jumping on board the competitiveness issue." The Bush regime and the doormat Congress have come together in the belief that the U.S. can keep its edge in science and technology if the federal government spends $9 billion a year to "fund innovative, big-payoff ideas that have the potential to transform the U.S. economy."

The utter stupidity of the "Protecting America's Competitive Edge Act" (PACE) is obvious. The tremendous labor cost advantage of doing things abroad will equally apply to any new "big-payoff ideas" as it does to the goods and services currently outsourced. Moreover, U.S. research is open-sourced. It is available to anyone. As the Cox Commission Report made clear, there are a large number of Chinese front companies in the U.S. for the sole purpose of collecting technology. PACE will simply be another U.S. taxpayer subsidy to the rising Asian economies.

The assertion that we hear every day that America is falling behind because it doesn't produce enough science, mathematics, and engineering graduates is a bald-faced lie. The problem is always brought back to education failures in K–12, that is, to more education subsidies. When CEOs say they can't find American engineers, they mean they cannot find Americans who will work for Chinese or Indian wages. That is what the so-called "shortage" is all about.

I receive a constant stream of emails from unemployed and underemployed engineers with many years of experience and advanced degrees. Many have been out of work for years. They describe the movement of their jobs offshore or their replacement by foreigners brought in on work visas. Many no longer even know American engineers who are employed in the profession. Some are now working in sawmills, others in Home Depot, and others are attempting to eke out a living as consultants. Many describe lost homes, broken marriages, even imprisonment for inability to make child support payments.

Many ask me how economists can be so blind to reality. Here is my answer: Many economists are bought and paid for by outsourcers. Most of the studies claiming to prove that Americans benefit from outsourcing are done by economic consulting firms hired by outsourcers. Or they are done by think tanks or university professors dependent on corporate donors. Or they reflect the ideology of "free market economists" who are committed to the belief that "freedom" is good and always produces good results. Since outsourcing is merely the freedom of property to act in its interest, and since this self-interest is always guided by an invisible hand to the greater welfare of everyone, outsourcing, ipso facto, is good for America. Anyone who doesn't think so is a fascist who wants to take away the rights of property. Seriously, this is what passes for analysis among "free market economists." Economists' commitment to their "reality" is destroying the ladders of upward mobility that made America the land of opportunity. It is just as destructive as the neocons' commitment to their "reality" that is driving the U.S. deeper into war in the Middle East.

Fact and analysis no longer play a role. The spun reality in which Americans live is insulated against intelligent perception.

American "manufacturers" are becoming merely marketers of foreign made goods. The CEOs and shareholders have too short a time horizon to understand that once foreigners control the manufacture-design-innovation process, they will bypass American brand names. U.S. companies will simply cease to exist.

Norm Augustine, former CEO of Lockheed Martin, says that even McDonald's jobs are no longer safe. Why pay an error-prone order-taker the minimum wage when McDonald's can have the order transmitted via satellite to a central location and from there to the person preparing the order. McDonald's experiment with this system to date has cut its error rate by 50 per cent and increased its throughput by 20 per cent.

Americans are giving up their civil liberties because they fear terrorist attacks. All of the terrorists in the world cannot do America the damage it has already suffered from offshore outsourcing.

FEBRUARY 16, 2006

CHAPTER 12

The Job Arbitrageurs: Partnering the Destruction of the American Economy

N March, 2005, the U.S. economy created a paltry 111,000 private sector jobs, half the expected amount. Following a well-established pattern, U.S. job growth was concentrated in domestic services: waitresses and bartenders, construction, administrative and waste services, and health care and social assistance.

In the 21st century the U.S. economy has ceased to create jobs in knowledge industries or information technology (IT). It has been a long time since any jobs were created in export and import-competitive sectors.

The Bureau of Labor Statistics forecasts no change in the new pattern of U.S. payroll job growth. Outsourcing and offshore production have reduced the need for American engineers, scientists, designers, accountants, stock analysts, and other professional skills. A college degree is no longer a ticket to upward mobility for Americans.

Nandan Nilekani is CEO of Infosys, an Indian software development firm. In an interview with *New Scientist* (Feb 19, 2005), he noted that outsourcing is causing American students to "stop studying technical subjects. They are already becoming wary of going into a field which will be 'Bangalored' tomorrow."

Bangalore is India's Silicon Valley. A 21st century creation of outsourcing, Bangalore is a new R&D home for Hewlett-Packard, GE, Google, Cisco, Intel, Sun Microsystems, Motorola, and Microsoft. The *New Scientist* reports: "The concentration of high-tech companies in the city is unparalleled almost anywhere in the world. At last count, Bangalore had more than 150,000 software engineers."

Meanwhile American software engineers go begging for employment, with several hundred thousand unemployed. I know engineers in their 30s with excellent experience who have been out of work since their jobs were outsourced four or five years ago. One is moving to Thailand to take a job in an outsourcing operation at $875 a month.

A country that permits its manufacturing and its technical and scientific professions to wither away is a country on a path to the Third World. The mark of a Third World country is a labor force employed in domestic services.

Many Americans and almost every economist and policymaker do not see the peril. They confuse outsourcing with free trade, and they have been taught that free trade is always beneficial.

Outsourcing is labor arbitrage. Cheaper foreign labor is being substituted for more expensive First World labor. Higher productivity no longer protects the wages and salaries of First World employees from cheap foreign labor. Political change in Asia has made it easy to move First World capital and technology to cheap labor, and the Internet has made it easy to move cheap labor to First World capital and technology. When working with First World capital and technology, foreign labor is just as productive—and a lot cheaper.

This is a new development. It is not a development covered by the case for free trade.

Outsourcing's apologists claim that it will create new jobs for Americans, but there is no sign of these jobs in the payroll jobs data. Moreover, it doesn't require much thought to see that the same incentive to outsource would apply to any such new jobs. By definition, outsourcing is the substitution of foreign labor for domestic labor. It is impossible for a process that replaces domestic employees with foreigners to create jobs for domestic labor.

Now biotech and pharmaceutical jobs and innovation itself are being moved offshore. The *Boston Globe* reports that Indian chemists with Ph.D. degrees work for one-fifth the pay of U.S. chemists. American chemists cannot give up 80 per cent of their pay to meet the competition and still pay their bills. Rising interest rates will make it difficult enough for Americans to make their mortgage payments, and the dollar's declining exchange value will raise the prices of the goods and services that have been moved offshore.

Americans are unaware of the difficult adjustments that are coming their way. By the time Americans catch on to outsourcing, its proponents will have changed its name to "strategic sourcing" or "partnering."

Corporations, economists, and politicians have written off American labor. No end of the job drought is in sight.

April 5, 2005

CHAPTER 13

No Jobs in the New or Old Economy

DECEMBER, 2008 DID NOT BRING AMERICANS ANY JOBS. TO THE contrary, the private sector lost 13,000 jobs from the previous month.

If December is a harbinger of the new year, it is going to be a bad one. The past year, hailed by Republican propagandists and "free trade" economists as proof of globalism's benefit to Americans, was dismal. According to the Bureau of Labor Statistics' nonfarm payroll data, the U.S. "super economy" created a miserable 1,054,000 net new jobs during 2007.

This is not enough to keep up with population growth—even at the rate discouraged Americans, unable to find jobs, are dropping out of the work force—thus the rise in the unemployment rate to 5 per cent.

During the past year, U.S. goods producing industries, continuing a long trend, lost 374,000 jobs.

But making things was the "old economy." The "new economy" provides services. Last year 1,428,000 private sector service jobs were created.

Are the "free trade" propagandists correct that these service jobs, which are our future, are high-end jobs in research and development, innovation, venture capitalism, information technology, high finance, and science and engineering where the U.S. allegedly has such a shortage of scientists and engineers that it must import them from abroad on work visas?

Not according to the official job statistics.

What occupations provided the 1.4 million service jobs in 2007?

Waitresses and bartenders accounted for 304,200, or 21 per cent of the new service jobs last year and 29 per cent of the net new jobs.

Health care and social assistance accounted for 478,400, or 33 per cent of the new service jobs and 45 per cent of the net new jobs. Ambulatory health care and hospitals accounted for the lion's share of these jobs.

Professional and business services accounted for 314,000, or 22 per cent of the new service jobs and 30 per cent of the net new jobs. Are these professional and business service jobs the high-end jobs of which "free traders" speak? Decide for yourself. Services to buildings and dwellings account for 53,600 of the jobs. Accounting and bookkeeping services account for 60,500 of the jobs. Architectural and engineering services account for 54,700 of the jobs. Computer systems design and related services account for 70,400 of the jobs. Management consultants account for 88,400 of the jobs.

There were more jobs for hospital orderlies than for architects and engineers. Waitresses and bartenders accounted for as many of last year's new jobs as the entirety of professional and business services.

Wholesale and retail trade, transportation, and utilities accounted for 181,000 of 2007's new jobs.

Where are the rest of the new jobs? There are a few scattered among arts, entertainment, and recreation, repair and maintenance, personal and laundry services, and membership associations and organizations.

That's it.

Keep in mind that the loss of 374,000 goods producing jobs must be subtracted from the 1,428,000 new service jobs to arrive at the net job gain figure. The new service jobs account for more than 100 per cent of the net new jobs.

Keep in mind, too, that many of the new jobs are not filled by American citizens. Many of the engineering and science jobs were filled by foreigners brought in on work visas. Indians and others from abroad can be hired to work in the U.S. for one-third less. The engineering and science jobs that are offshored are paid as little as one-fifth of the U.S. salary. Even foreign nurses are brought in on work visas. No one knows how many of the hospital orderlies are illegals.

What a super "new economy" Americans have! U.S. job growth has a distinctly Third World flavor. A very small per centage of 2007's new jobs required a college education. Since there are so few jobs for university graduates, how is "education the answer"?

Where is the benefit to Americans of offshoring? The answer is that the benefit is confined to a few highly paid executives who receive multi-million dollar bonuses for increasing profits by offshoring jobs. The rest of the big money went to Wall Street crooks who sold trusting people subprime derivatives.

"Free traders" will assert that the benefit is in low Wal-Mart prices. But the prices are low only because China keeps its currency pegged to the dollar. Thus, the Chinese currency value falls with the dollar. The peg will not continue forever. The dollar has lost 40 per cent of its value against the Euro during the years of the Bush regime. Already China is having to adjust the peg. When the peg goes, Wal-Mart shoppers will think they are in Neiman Marcus.

Just as Americans have been betrayed by "their" leaders in government at all levels, they have been betrayed by business "leaders" on Wall Street and in the corporations. U.S. government and business elites have proven themselves to be Americans' worst enemies.

JANUARY 8, 2008

CHAPTER 14

The Great American Job Sell-Out

AMERICANS ARE BEING SOLD OUT ON THE JOBS FRONT. Americans' employment opportunities are declining as a result of corporate outsourcing of U.S. jobs, H-1B visas that import foreigners to displace Americans in their own country, and federal guest worker programs.

President Bush and his Republican majority intend to legalize the aliens who hold down wages for construction companies and cleaning services. In order to stretch budgets, state and local governments bring in lower paid foreign nurses and school teachers. To reduce costs, U.S. corporations outsource jobs abroad and use work visa programs to import foreign engineers and programmers. The American job give away is explained by a "shortage" of Americans to take the jobs.

There are not too many Americans willing to accept the pay and working conditions of migrant farm workers. However, the U.S. is bursting at the seams with unemployed computer engineers and well-educated professionals who are displaced by outsourcing and H-1B visas. During Bush's entire first term, there was a net loss of American private sector jobs. Today there are 760,000 fewer private sector jobs in the U.S. economy than when Bush was first inaugurated in January 2001.

For years the hallmark of the European economy was its inability to create any jobs other than government jobs. America has caught up with Europe. During Bush's first term, state and local government created 879,000 new government jobs. Offsetting these government jobs against the net loss in private sector jobs gives Bush a four-year jobs growth of 119,000 government jobs. Comparing this pathetic result to normal performance produces a shortage of millions of U.S. jobs. What happened to these jobs?

Over these same four years the composition of U.S. jobs has changed from higher-paid manufacturing and information technology jobs to lower-paid domestic services. Why?

During this extraordinary breakdown in the American employment machine, politicians, government officials, corporate spokespersons, and "free trade" economists gave assurances that America was benefitting greatly from the work visa programs and outsourcing.

The mindless chatter continues. Just the other day Ambassador David Gross, U.S. Coordinator for International Communications and Information Policy in the State Department, declared outsourcing to be an economic efficiency that works to America's benefit. There is no sign of this alleged benefit in U.S. jobs statistics or the U.S. balance of trade.

Repeatedly and incorrectly, U.S. corporations state that outsourcing creates more U.S. jobs. They even convinced a *New York Times* columnist that this was the case.

The problem is, no one can identify where the U.S. jobs are that outsourcing allegedly creates. They are certainly not to be found in the BLS jobs statistics. However, the Indian and Chinese jobs created by U.S. outsourcing are highly visible.

On February 13, the *Dayton Daily News* (Ohio) reported that jobs outsourcing is transforming Indian "cities like Bangalore from sleepy little backwaters into the New York Cities of Asia." In a very short period outsourcing has helped to raise India from one of the world's poorest countries to its seventh largest economy.

Outsourcing proponents claim that U.S. job loss is being exaggerated, that outsourcing is really just a small thing involving a few call centers. If that is the case, how is it transforming sleepy Indian cities into "the New York Cities of Asia"? If outsourcing is no big deal, why are Bangalore hotel rooms "packed with foreigners paying rates higher than in Tokyo or London," as the *Dayton Daily News* reports?

If outsourcing is of no real consequence, why are American lawyers or their clients paying $2,900 in fees plus hotel and travel expenses and two days' billings to attend the Fourth National Conference on Outsourcing in Financial Services in Washington, D.C. (April 20–21)?

On the jobs front, as on the war front, the Social Security front, and every other front, Americans are not being given the truth. Americans' news comes from people allied with the Bush administration or dependent on revenues from corporate advertisers. Displease the government or advertisers and your media empire is in trouble. The news most Americans get is filtered. It is the permitted news. Many "free trade" advocates also are dependent on the corporate money that funds their salaries, research, and think tanks.

Another clear indication that outsourcing of U.S. jobs is no small thing comes from the reported earnings of the leading Indian corporations that provide American firms with outsourced IT employees and engineers. During the recent quarter, Ifosys' revenues increased by 53 per cent, TCS grew by 38 per cent, and Wipro was up 34 per cent.

On January 1, 2001, Cincinnati-based Convergys Corp had one Indian employee. Today it has 10,000. Why? Because it can hire Indian university graduates for $240 a month, a sum that is a fraction of the U.S. poverty level income.

Many Americans think that an outsourced job is an existing job that is moved offshore. But many outsourced jobs are created offshore in the first place. On February 11, *USA Today* told the story of OfficeTiger, "the sort of young technology company that once created thousands of high-paying jobs in the U.S.A, fueling sizzling economic growth." The five-year-old startup business employs 200 Americans and ten times that number of Indians. The company has plans for hiring many more Indians to perform "tech-heavy financial services."

Under pressure from venture capitalists who fund new companies, American startup firms are starting up abroad. Thus, the new ventures, which "free trade" economists assured us would create new jobs to take the place of the ones moved offshore by mature firms, are in fact creating jobs for foreigners.

As a consequence, tech jobs in the U.S. are falling as a per centage of the total. Clearly, tax breaks for venture capitalists are self defeating when the result is to create jobs for foreigners, not for Americans. Why should the American taxpayer subsidize employment in India and China?

These developments have obvious adverse implications for engineering and professional education in America. The BLS jobs forecast for the next ten years says the vast majority of U.S. jobs will not require a college education. University enrollments will decline and so will the production of Ph.Ds as fewer professors are needed.

As India and China rise to First World status, the U.S. falls to Third World status where the only jobs are in domestic services.

This has enormous implications for the U.S. balance of payments. Americans' consumption of manufactured goods is heavily dependent on foreign manufacture, whether that of foreign firms or that of U.S. multinational firms that supply their American customers from offshore. How does an economy in which employment growth is concentrated in nontradable domestic services pay for its imports with exports?

Since 1990 the U.S. has been paying for its imports by giving foreigners ownership of its assets. In the last 15 years foreigners have accumulated $3.6 trillion of America's wealth.

America has been able to pay for its consumption by giving up its wealth because the dollar is the world's reserve currency. As America's high-tech and manufacturing capabilities decline and its red ink rises, the dollar's role as reserve currency must end.

When the dollar loses its reserve currency role, America will not be able to pay for the imports on which it has become dependent.

Until recent years, U.S. companies employed Americans to produce the goods that Americans consumed. Employment supported sales, and sales supported employment. No more. By their shortsighted policy of moving U.S. jobs abroad, our corporations are destroying their American markets.

Economists give assurances that the dollar's decline and fall will bring jobs and industry back to the U.S. Once Americans are as poor as Indians and Chinese are today, the process will reverse. Multinational corporations will locate in America to take advantage of cheap labor and unserved markets. By becoming poor, the U.S. can become rich again.

You might want to ask the economists and our "leaders" in Washington why we should put ourselves and our descendants through such a wrenching process.

FEBRUARY 15, 2005

CHAPTER 15

Economists in Denial

AT A WASHINGTON, D.C. PRESS CONFERENCE LAST NOVEMBER, Harvard University professor Michael Porter claimed that globalism was bringing benefits to Americans (*Manufacturing & Technology News*, Nov. 30, 2006). Porter was introducing the latest report, "Competitiveness Index: Where America Stands" of which he is a principal author, from the Council on Competitiveness.

I recognized a number of Porter's claims to be inconsistent with empirical data. After examining the report, I can confidently state that the report provides scant evidence that America is benefiting from globalism.

This is not to say that the statements in the report and the information in the numerous charts are untrue. It is to say that the data do not support the claim that America is benefiting from globalism.

The competitiveness report boasts that the United States "leads all major economies in GDP per capita"; that "household wealth grew strongly, supported by gains in real estate and stocks"; and that "poverty rates improved for all groups over the past two decades."

All of this is true over the time periods that the report measures.

But it is also true that all of this was happening prior to globalism. Moreover, in recent years as globalism becomes more pronounced, the U.S. economy is performing less well.

The report provides no information that would suggest that the gains measured over 20 years or more occurred because of globalism or that the economy is performing better today than in past periods.

Indeed, the report acknowledges under-performance in critical areas.

U.S. job creation in the 21st century is below past performance. Debt payments of Americans as a per cent of their disposable incomes are rising while the savings rate has collapsed into dis-saving. Poverty rates have turned back up in the 21st century when the impact of globalism on Americans has been most pronounced.

A total critique of the competitiveness report would be as long, or longer, than the report's 100 pages. As this is beyond the permissible length of an article and readers' patience, I will limit my remarks to the most critical issues.

The report mentions many times that the United States is the driver of global growth without emphasizing that U.S. growth is debt-driven. Both the U.S. government and U.S. consumers are accumulating debt at a rapid pace. Debt-driven consumption is exceeding U.S. output by a sum in excess of $800 billion annually.

The trade and current account deficits are rapidly increasing the burden of debt service on Americans and threatening the dollar's role as reserve currency. The competitiveness report makes these negatives sound like America is leading the world by driving economic growth.

In the middle of the report there is a misleading chart that shows that "U.S.A. attracts most foreign direct investment"—in terms of dollars. The report asserts that "the United States remains a magnet for global investment" because of "America's high levels of productivity, strong growth and unparalleled consumer market."

This is one of the instances in which the report becomes totally propagandistic.

The report suggests, as do many careless economists, that foreign direct investment in the U.S. consists of new plant and equipment, which, in turn, is creating jobs for Americans. However, foreign direct investment in the United States consists almost entirely of foreign acquisitions of existing U.S. assets. Foreign direct investment is merely the counterpart of the huge American trade and current account deficits. America pays for its over-consumption in dollars which foreigners use to buy up existing U.S. assets. One result is that the income streams associated with the change of ownership now accrue to foreigners and, thereby, worsen the current account deficit.

The chart below on foreign direct investment cannot be found in the competitiveness report. It is provided by Charles McMillion of MBG Information Services in Washington, D.C. The chart makes it completely clear that foreign direct investment in the United States consists of foreign acquisition of existing U.S. assets. Foreign acquisition of existing U.S. assets hurts America by diverting income streams to foreigners.

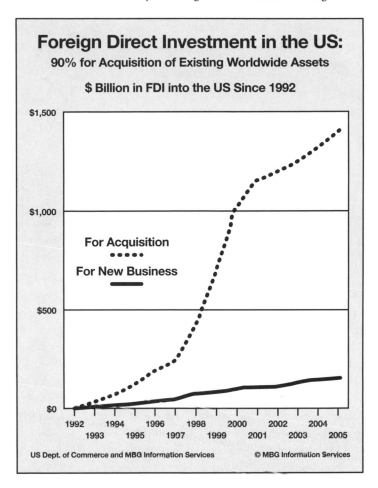

Foreign Direct Investment in the US:
90% for Acquisition of Existing Worldwide Assets

$ Billion in FDI into the US Since 1992

For Acquisition

For New Business

US Dept. of Commerce and MBG Information Services   © MBG Information Services

Another fantastic error in Porter's report is the misleading claims about U.S. productivity growth. There is no chart in the report, such as the one provided by McMillion, that shows the extraordinary and widening divergence of U.S. productivity from real compensation.

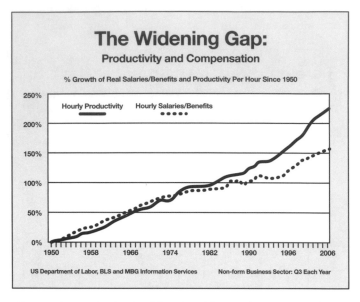

Economists maintain that labor is paid according to its productivity, and historically this has been the case in the United States. The correlation began to break down with the advent of offshoring to the Asian Tigers and deteriorated further with the advent of offshoring of manufacturing and service jobs to China and India made possible by the collapse of world socialism and the advent of the high-speed Internet. The historical correlation between productivity and wages has been further eroded by the importation into the United States of cheap foreign skilled labor on work visas. Many Americans have been forced to train their foreign replacements who work for one-third less pay.

The greatest failure in the competitiveness report is the absence of mention of the labor arbitrage and its consequences when U.S. firms offshore their production for U.S. markets. This practice translates into direct job loss and direct tax base loss, and it transforms domestic output into imports. This is capital and technology chasing absolute advantage abroad. This cannot be considered trade based on resources finding their comparative advantage in the domestic economy.

It is this replacement of U.S. employees by foreign workers that explains the extraordinary rise in CEO compensation and the flow of most of the income and wealth gains to the few people at the top. By off-shoring their workforces, CEOs cut their costs and make or exceed their earnings forecasts, thus receiving bonuses that are many multiples of their salaries. Shareholders also benefit. When plants are closed and jobs are offshored, American employees lose their livelihoods, but managements and shareholders prosper. Offshoring is causing an extraordinary increase in American income inequality.

The report acknowledges that "for the first time in history, emerging economies, such as China, are loaning enormous amounts of money to the world's richest country." Historically, it was rich countries that lent to underdeveloped countries. The truth of the matter is that China's loans to the United States are a form of forced lending. China is flooded with dollars from America's dependency on imports of Chinese manufactures and advanced technology products. There is nothing that China can do with the dollars except to purchase existing U.S. equity assets or lend the dollars back to the United States by purchasing Treasury debt. With China's currency pegged to the dollar, China cannot dump the dollars into foreign exchange markets without initiating a run on the dollar and complaints that China is increasing its competitive advantage over the rest of the world.

When I was Assistant Secretary of the U.S. Treasury in the early 1980s, U.S. foreign assets exceeded foreign-owned assets in the United States. By 2005 this had changed dramatically, with foreigners owning $2.7 trillion more of the U.S. than the U.S. owns abroad. For the first time since the United States was a developing country 90 years ago, the country is paying more to foreign creditors than it is receiving from its investments abroad.

The report downplays the extraordinary trade and current account deficits on the grounds that "foreign affiliate sales" do not count against the trade deficit and "intra-firm trade" is a significant proportion of the trade deficit and "is due to trade within American companies."

This argument shows that the report is written from the standpoint of what is good for global firms, not what is good for America.

It made some sense when General Motors claimed that what is good for General Motors is good for America, because when the claim was made General Motors produced in America with American labor. It makes no sense to make this claim today when what is good for a company is achieved at the expense of the American work force.

"Intra-firm trade" is simply a company's products and inputs produced in its offshore plants, and "foreign affiliate sales" is simply a company's overseas earnings from its production in foreign countries with foreign labor.

Perhaps Porter is arguing that the output of an American subsidiary in Germany, for example, should be considered part of U.S. GDP. Such an accounting would result in a magical increase in U.S. GDP and drop in German GDP. If success is defined in terms of the country in which the ownership of the profits of global firms resides, only then a country can be successful with its labor force unemployed.

The competitiveness report owes much of its failure to an abstraction—"the global labor supply." There is no global labor market that equilibrates wages in the different countries. There are only national labor markets in which wages reflect cost of living and labor supply.

For example, in China, the cost of living is low, and excess supplies of labor suppress manufacturing wages below the productivity of labor. In the United States, the cost of living and debt levels are high, and the labor market (except for those parts hardest hit by offshoring) is not confronted with large excess supplies of labor. It is possible for a U.S.-based firm to hire someone living in China or India to deliver services over the Internet at a fraction of the cost of hiring an American employee. Alternatively, foreigners can be brought in on work visas to replace American employees. Manufacturing plants can be moved abroad where excess supplies of labor keep wages far below productivity. These are all examples of capital seeking absolute advantage in lowest factor cost.

The report makes the false claim that the future of U.S. competitiveness depends on education. Although the United States has 17 of the world's top 20 best research universities, Porter sees education as the number-one weakness of the U.S. economic system. The report envisions a high-wage service economy based on imagination and ingenuity.

Here the competitiveness report fails big time, because it fails to comprehend that all tradable services can be offshored.

In the 21st century, the U.S. economy has been able to create net new jobs only in non-tradable domestic services. The vast majority of jobs in the BLS ten-year jobs projections do not require a college education. The problem in 21st century America is not a lack of educated people, but a lack of jobs for educated people.

Many American software engineers and IT professionals have been forced by jobs offshoring to abandon their professions. The November 6, 2006 issue of *Chemical & Engineering News* reports that "the per centage of American Chemical Society member chemists in the domestic workforce who did not have full-time jobs as of March of this year was 8.7 per cent." There is no reason for Americans to pursue education in science and technology when career opportunities in those fields are declining due to offshoring.

Porter says the future for America cannot be found in manufacturing or tradable goods, but only in what he says are high-wage service skills in "expert thinking" and "complex communication." The report does not identify these jobs, and scant sign of them can be found in the BLS jobs data.

Princeton University economist Alan Blinder, former vice chairman of the Federal Reserve, writes that "we have so far barely seen the tip of the offshoring iceberg, the eventual dimensions of which may be staggering" (*Dallas Morning News*, January 7, 2007). Elsewhere, Blinder has estimated that as many as 50 million jobs in tradable services are at risk of being offshored to lower-paid foreigners.

Like Porter, Blinder says that America's future lies in service jobs. The good service jobs will be those delivering "creativity and imagination." Blinder understands that the education solution might be a pipe dream as such abilities "are notoriously difficult to teach in schools." Blinder also understands that "it is hard to imagine that truly creative positions will ever constitute anything close to the majority of jobs." Blinder asks: "What will everyone else do?"

Blinder acknowledges that considering the wage differentials between the United States and India, Americans will find employment only in services that are not deliverable electronically, such as janitors and crane operators. These hands-on service jobs do "not correspond to traditional distinctions between jobs that require high levels of education and jobs that do not."

Blinder's prediction of the future of American employment is in line with my own and that of the Bureau of Labor Statistics. Where Blinder falls down is in not seeing the implication of these trends on the U.S. trade deficit. A country whose workforce is employed in domestic non-tradable services is a Third World country with nothing to export. How will the United States pay for its heavy dependence on imports of manufactured goods and energy?

As long as the dollar retains its reserve currency role, Americans can continue to hand over paper for real goods and services. But how long can the United States retain the reserve currency role when its economy does not make things to export, when its work force is employed in domestic services, and when its foreign creditors own its assets?

Blinder, like Porter and almost every other economist, warns against trying to prevent America's descent into a Third World existence. Blinder says protection would block trade and "probably do a great deal of harm." But both Blinder and the competitiveness report show a great deal of harm being done to Americans by offshoring the production of goods and services for American markets. As more and more high value-added U.S. occupations in tradable services are undercut by offshoring, the ladders of upward mobility that made America a land of opportunity are taken down. As the bulk of domestic service jobs do not require a university education, the United States will find itself over-invested in educational institutions and decline will set in.

For developed economies, offshoring is a reversal of the development process. As offshoring progresses, the domestic economy will become less developed and have less demand for university education.

Economists cannot speak the obvious truth, because they mistake the operation of absolute advantage for comparative advantage. The case for free trade rests on the comparative advantage argument that countries that specialize in what they do best and trade for goods that other countries do best share in the gains from trade and experience higher standards of living.

In 2000, the case for free trade came under powerful attack when MIT Press published *Global Trade and Conflicting National Interests* by Ralph Gomory and William Baumol. This work shows that the case for free trade has been incorrect since the day David Ricardo made it. Economists have not come to terms with this important work, and they will resist doing so for as long as they can as it demolishes their human capital.

The challenging work by Gomory and Baumol aside, I have shown, as has Herman Daly, that the two conditions on which comparative advantage depends no longer hold in the present-day world. One condition is that capital must be immobile internationally and seek its comparative advantage in the domestic economy, not move across international borders in search of lowest factor cost. The other condition is that countries have different relative cost ratios of producing tradable goods.

Today, capital is as mobile internationally as tradable goods, and knowledge-based production functions operate identically regardless of location. Neither of the conditions upon which the case for free trade rests exists in the present-day world.

As the necessary conditions for the free-trade case no longer exist, and if the case for free trade has been wrong from the beginning as Gomory and Baumol indicate, then America's free trade policy rests in fantastic error.

Economists long ago ceased to think objectively about free trade. Free trade has become an unexamined article of faith. As far as I can ascertain, economists no longer are even aware of the necessary conditions specified by Ricardo that are the basis for the free trade case.

Economists have made a number of blunders in their arguments seeking to protect offshoring from criticism. For example, Matthew Slaughter, a member of President Bush's Council of Economic Advisors, penned a study that concluded: "For every one job that U.S. multinationals created abroad in their foreign affiliates, they created nearly two U.S. jobs in their parent operations." How did Slaughter arrive at this conclusion—a conclusion that can find no support in the BLS jobs data?

Slaughter reached his incorrect conclusion by failing to take into account the two reasons for the increase in multinational employment. One is that multinationals acquired many existing smaller firms, thus raising multinational employment but not overall employment. The other is that many U.S. firms established foreign operations for the first time and thereby became multinationals, thus adding their existing employment to Slaughter's number for multinational employees.

Another problem is that the corruption of the outside world has found its way into universities. Today, universities look upon "name" professors as rainmakers who bring in funds from well-heeled interest groups. Increasingly, research and reports serve the interests that finance them and not the truth. Money rules, and professors who bring money to universities find it increasingly difficult to avoid serving the agendas of donors.

When a country gives up producing tradable goods, it gives up the occupations associated with manufacturing. Engineering and R&D move away with the manufacturing. It is impossible to innovate independently of the manufacturing and R&D base. Innovation is based on state-of-the-art knowledge of what is being done, and if the doing is done elsewhere, the would-be innovator will find himself at a disadvantage.

Offshoring is causing dire problems for the United States. I have suggested that one necessary reform will be to break the connection between CEO pay and short-run profit performance. As long as CEOs can get filthy rich in a few years by dumping their U.S. workforce, the trade deficit will continue to rise, and more college graduates will be employed as waitresses and bartenders.

The short-run time horizon of U.S. management endangers the long-term viability of U.S. firms. This short-run time horizon is the result of a "reform" that sought to give investors the most up-to-date financial information. The reformers did not consider the unintended consequences of quarterly reporting.

To level the playing field for American labor, Ralph Gomory suggests that U.S. corporations be taxed not on income but on the per centage of the value added to their output that occurs in the U.S. Companies that produce in the U.S. would have low tax rates; companies that produce abroad would have high tax rates.

Economists need to inject some realism into their dogmas. The U.S. economy did not develop on the basis of free trade. Whatever the costs of protection, the costs did not prevent America's economic rise.

Much American economic thinking is grounded in the fact of America's past success. Many economists take it for granted that as long as the U.S. has free markets, it will continue to be successful. However, much of America's success is due to World War I and World War II, which bankrupted rivals and destroyed their industrial capacity. It was easy for the United States to dominate world trade after World War II as America was the only country with an intact economy.

Many economists dismiss the problems with which offshoring confronts developed economies with the argument that it is just a question of wage equilibration. As wages rise in China and India, the labor cost differential will disappear and wages will be the same everywhere. This argument overlooks the lengthy period required for the hundreds of millions of workers, who overhang labor markets in India and China to be absorbed into the workforce. During this time, hardships in currently high-wage countries will be severe. Moreover, once the wage adjustment is complete, the new developed countries will have the upper hand. Will they give up their competitive and strategic advantages?

In the July 2006 issue of *CounterPunch*, I wrote that jobs offshoring was the new form of class warfare and that it was bringing political instability and social strife to the United States. There is nothing in the Council on Competitiveness' latest report to cause me to alter my view.

FEBRUARY 19, 2007

CHAPTER 16

How the Economic News is Spun

READERS ASK ME TO RECONCILE THE JOBS AND DEBT DATA THAT I report to them with the positive economic outlook and good news that comes to them from regular news sources. Some readers are being snide, but most are sincere.

I am pleased to provide the explanation. First, let me give my reassurances that the numbers I report to you come straight from official U.S. government statistics. I do not massage the numbers or rework them in any way. I cannot assure you that the numbers are perfectly reported to, and collected by, the government, but they are the only numbers we have.

Here is how to reconcile my reports with the good news you get from the mainstream media:

(1) When the U.S. Department of Labor, for example, releases the monthly payroll jobs data, the press release will put the best spin on the data. The focus is on the aggregate number of new jobs created the previous month, for example, 150,000 new jobs. That sounds good. News reporters report the press release. They do not look into the data to see what kinds of jobs have been created and what kinds are being lost. They do not look back in time and provide a net job creation number over a longer period of time.

This is why the American public is unaware that higher paid jobs in export and import-competitive industries are being phased out along with engineering and other professional "knowledge jobs" and replaced with lower-paid jobs in domestic services. The replacement of higher paid jobs with lower-paid jobs is one reason for the decline in median household income over the past five years. It is not a large decline, but it is a decline. How can it be possible for the economy to be doing well when median household income is not growing and when economic growth is based on increased consumer indebtedness?

Economists, comfortable with their free trade ideology, are simply careless with data. Remember Matthew Slaughter's error. He concluded that "for every one job that U.S. multinationals created abroad in their foreign affiliates they created nearly two U.S. jobs in the parent operations." Slaughter arrived at this erroneous conclusion by counting the growth in multinational jobs in the U.S. without adjusting the data to reflect the acquisition of existing firms by multinationals and for existing firms turning themselves into multinationals by establishing foreign operations for the first time. There was no new employment in the U.S. Existing employment simply moved into the multinational category from a change in the status of firms to multinational.

(2) Wall Street economists are salesmen. The companies that employ them want to sell stocks and bonds. They don't want bad news. A bear market is not good for business. Similarly, business associations have the agenda of their members. Offshore outsourcing reduces their labor costs and boosts their profits and performance-based bonuses. Therefore, it is natural that their association reports put a positive spin on outsourcing. The same organizations benefit from work visas that allow them to bring foreign workers in as indentured servants to replace their more fractious and higher paid American employees. Thus, the myth of a U.S. shortage of engineers and scientists. This myth is used to wheedle more subsidies in the form of more H-1B visas out of Congress.

(3) Official U.S. government reports are written to obfuscate serious problems for which the government has no solution. For example, "The Economic Report of the President," written by the Council of Economic Advisers, blames the huge U.S. trade deficit on the low rate of domestic savings. The report claims that if only Americans would save more of their incomes, they would not spend so much on imports, and the $726 billion trade gap would close.

This analysis is nonsensical on its face. Offshore outsourcing has turned U.S. production into imports. Americans are now dependent on offshore production for their clothes, manufactured goods, and advanced technology products. There are simply no longer domestic producers of many of the products on which Americans depend.

Moreover, many Americans are struggling to make ends meet, having lost their jobs to offshore outsourcing. They are living on credit cards and struggling to make minimum payments. Median household real incomes are falling as higher paid jobs are outsourced while Americans are relegated to lower-paying jobs in domestic services.

They haven't a dollar to save. As Charles McMillion points out, the February 28, 2006, report from the Bureau of Economic Analysis shows that all GDP growth in the fourth quarter of 2005 was due to the accumulation of unsold inventory and that consumers continued to outspend their incomes.

Matthew Spiegleman, a Conference Board economist, claims that manufacturing jobs are only slightly higher paid than domestic service jobs. He reaches this conclusion by comparing only hourly pay and by leaving out the longer manufacturing work week and the associated benefits, such as health care and pensions.

(4) Policy reports from think tanks reflect what the donors want to hear. Truth can be "negative" and taken as a reflection on the favored administration in power. Consider, for example, the conservative, Bruce Bartlett, who was recently fired by the National Center for Policy Analysis for writing a truthful book about George W. Bush's economic policies. Donors to NCPA saw Bartlett's truthful book as an attack on George Bush, their hero, and withheld $165,000 in donations. There were not enough Bartlett supporters to step in and fill the gap, so he was fired in order to save donations.

When I held the William E. Simon Chair in Political Economy at the Center for Strategic and International Studies, I saw internal memos describing the grants CSIS could receive from the George H.W. Bush administration in exchange for removing me from the Simon chair.

In America "truth" has long been for sale. We see it in expert witness testimony, in the corrupt reports from forensic labs that send innocent people to prison, and even in policy disputes among scientists themselves. In scholarship, ideas that are too challenging to prevailing opinion have a rough row to hoe and often cannot get a hearing.

The few reporters and columnists who are brave or naive enough to speak out are constrained by editors who are constrained by owners and advertisers.

All of these reasons and others make truth a scarce commodity. Censorship exists everywhere and is especially heavy in the U.S. mainstream media.

MARCH 3, 2006

CHAPTER 17

The Science & Technology Jobs Shortage Myth

I N JUNE, 2007, A REVEALING MARKETING VIDEO FROM THE LAW FIRM Cohen & Grigsby appeared on the Internet. The video demonstrated the law firm's techniques for getting around U.S. law governing work visas in order to enable corporate clients to replace their American employees with foreigners who work for less. The law firm's marketing manager, Lawrence Lebowitz, is upfront with interested clients: "our goal is clearly not to find a qualified and interested U.S. worker."

If an American somehow survives the weeding out process, "have the manager of that specific position step in and go through the whole process to find a legal basis to disqualify them for this position—in most cases there doesn't seem to be a problem."

No problem for the employer he means, only for the expensively educated American university graduate who is displaced by a foreigner imported on a work visa justified by a nonexistent shortage of trained and qualified Americans.

University of California computer science professor Norm Matloff, who watches this issue closely, said that Cohen & Grigsby's practices are the standard ones used by hordes of attorneys, who are cleaning up by putting Americans out of work.

The Cohen & Grigsby video was a short-term sensation as it undermined the business propaganda that no American employee was being displaced by foreigners on H 1B or L-1 work visas. Soon, however, business organizations and their shills were back in gear lying to Congress and the public about the amazing shortage of qualified Americans for literally every technical and professional occupation, especially IT and software engineering.

Everywhere we hear the same droning lie from business interests that there are not enough American engineers and scientists. For mysterious reasons Americans with university degrees prefer to be waitresses and bartenders, hospital orderlies, and retail clerks.

As one of the few who writes about this short-sighted policy of American managers endeavoring to maximize their "performance bonuses," I receive much feedback from affected Americans. Many responses come from recent university graduates such as the one who "graduated nearly at the top of my class in 2002" with degrees in both electrical and computer engineering and who "hasn't been able to find a job."

A college roommate of a family member graduated from a good engineering school last year with a degree in software engineering. He had one job interview. Jobless, he is back at home living with his parents and burdened with student loans that bought an education that offshoring and work visas have made useless to Americans.

The hundreds of individual cases that have been brought to my attention are dismissed as "anecdotal" by my fellow economists. So little do they know. I also receive numerous responses from American engineers and IT workers who have managed to hold on to jobs or to find new ones after long intervals when they have been displaced by foreign hires. Their descriptions of their work environments are fascinating.

For example, Dayton, Ohio was once home to numerous American engineers. Today, writes one surviving American, "I feel like an alien in my own country—as if Dayton had been colonized by India. NCR and other local employers have either offshored most of their IT work or rely heavily on Indian guest workers. The IT department of National City Bank across the street from LexisNexis is entirely Indian. The nearby apartment complexes house large numbers of Indian guest workers filling the engineering needs of many area businesses."

I have learned that Reed Elsevier, which owns LexisNexis, has hired a new Indian vice president for offshoring and that now the jobs of the Indian guest workers may be on the verge of being offshored to another country. The relentless drive for cheap labor now threatens the foreign guest workers who displaced America's own engineers.

One software engineer wrote to me protesting the ignorance of Thomas Friedman for creating a false picture of American engineers being outdated and for "denouncing American engineers and other workers as 'xenophobes' for opposing their displacement by foreign guest workers." The engineer also took exception to the "willful ignorance or cynicism" of pundits who he described as "bootlicks for pro-outsourcing lobbies."

On November 6, 2006, Michael S. Teitelbaum, vice president of the Alfred P. Sloan Foundation, explained to a subcommittee of the House Committee on Science and Technology the difference between the conventional or false portrait that there is a shortage of U.S. scientists and engineers and the reality on the ground. The reality is that offshoring, foreign guest workers, and educational subsidies have produced a surplus of U.S. engineers and scientists that leaves many facing unstable and failed careers.

As two examples of the false portrait, Teitelbaum cited the 2005 report, *Tapping America's Potential*, led by the Business Roundtable and signed onto by 14 other business associations, and the 2006 National Academies of Science report, *Rising Above the Gathering Storm*, "which was the basis for substantial parts of what eventually evolved into the American COMPETES Act."

Teitelbaum posed the question to the U.S. Representatives: "Why do you continue to hear energetic reassertions of the conventional portrait of 'shortages,' shortfalls, failures of K–12 science and math teaching, declining interest among U.S. students, and the necessity of importing more foreign scientists and engineers?"

Teitelbaum's answer: "In my judgment, what you are hearing is simply the expressions of interests by interest groups and their lobbyists. This phenomenon is, of course, very familiar to everyone on the Hill. Interest groups that are well organized and funded have the capacity to make their claims heard by you, either directly or via echoes in the mass press. Meanwhile those who are not well-organized and funded can express their views, but only as individuals."

Among the interest groups that benefit from the false portrait are universities, which gain graduate student enrollments and inexpensive postdocs to conduct funded lab research. Employers gain larger profits from lower paid scientists and engineers, and immigration lawyers gain fees by leading employers around the work visa rules.

Using the biomedical research sector as an example, Teitelbaum explained to the congressmen how research funding creates an oversupply of scientists that requires ever larger funding to keep employed. Teitelbaum made it clear that it is nonsensical to simultaneously increase the supply of American scientists while forestalling their employment with a shortage myth that is used to import foreigners on work visas.

Teitelbaum recommends that American students considering majors in science and engineering first investigate the career prospects of recent graduates.

Integrity is so lacking in America that the shortage myth serves the interests of universities, funding agencies, employers, and immigration attorneys at the expense of American students who naively pursue professions in which their prospects are dim. Initially it was blue-collar factory workers who were abandoned by U.S. corporations and politicians. Now it is white-collar employees and Americans trained in science and technology. Princeton University economist Alan Blinder estimates that there are tens of millions of American high end service jobs that ultimately face offshoring.

As I predict, and as BLS payroll jobs data indicate, in 20 years the U.S. will have a Third World work force engaged in domestic nontradable services.

DECEMBER 4, 2007

CHAPTER 18

Shrinking the U.S. Dollar From the Inside-Out

O N DECEMBER 8, 2007, CHINESE AND FRENCH NEWS SERVICES reported that Iran had stopped billing its oil exports in dollars. Americans might never hear this news as the independence of the U.S. media was destroyed in the 1990s when Rupert Murdoch persuaded the Clinton administration and the quislings in Congress to allow the U.S. media to be monopolized by a few mega-corporations.

Iran's oil minister, Gholam Hossein Nozari, declared: "The dollar is an unreliable currency in regards to its devaluation and the loss oil exporters have endured from this trend." Iran has proposed to OPEC that the U.S. dollar no longer be used by any oil exporting countries. As the oil emirates and the Saudis have already decided to reduce their holdings of U.S. dollars, the U.S. might actually find itself having to pay for its energy imports in euros or yen.

Venezuela's Chavez, survivor of a U.S.-led coup against him and a likely target of a U.S. assassination attempt, might follow the Iranian lead. Also, Russia's Putin, who is fed up with the U.S. government's efforts to encircle Russia militarily, will be tempted to add Russia's oil exports to the symbolic assault on the dollar.

The assault is symbolic, because the dollar is not the reserve currency due to oil exports being billed in dollars. It's the other way around. Oil exports are billed in dollars, because the dollar is the reserve currency.

What is important to the dollar's value and its role as reserve currency is whether foreigners continue to consider dollar-denominated assets sufficiently attractive to absorb the constant flow of red ink from U.S. trade and budget deficits. If Iran and other countries do not want dollars, they can exchange them for other currencies regardless of the currency in which oil is billed.

Indeed, the evidence is that foreigners are not finding dollar-denominated assets sufficiently attractive. The dollar has declined dramatically during the Bush regime regardless of the fact that oil is billed in dollars. Iran's remarks about the dollar is a market response to a depreciating currency, not a punitive action by Iran to sink the dollar.

Oil bills are only a small part of the problem. Oil minister Nozari's statement about the loss suffered by oil exporters applies to all exporters of all products.

A quarter century ago U.S. oil imports accounted for the U.S. trade deficit. The concerns expressed over the years about "energy dependence" accustomed Americans to think of trade problems only in terms of oil. The desire to gain "energy independence" has led to such foolish policies as subsidies for ethanol, the main effect of which is to drive up food prices and further ravage the poor.

Today oil imports comprise a small part of the U.S. trade deficit. During the decades when Americans were fixated on "the energy deficit," the U.S. became three times more dependent on foreign made manufactures. America's trade deficit in manufactured goods, including advanced technology products, dwarfs the U.S. energy deficit.

For example, the U.S. trade deficit with China is more than twice the size of the U.S. trade deficit with OPEC. The U.S. deficit with Japan is about the size of the U.S. deficit with OPEC. With an overall U.S. trade deficit of more than $800 billion, the deficit with OPEC only comprises one-eighth.

If abandonment of the dollar by oil exporters is not the cause of the dollar's woes, what is?

There are two reasons for the dollar's demise. One is the practice of American corporations offshoring their production for U.S. consumers. When U.S. corporations move to foreign countries their production of goods and services for American consumers, they convert U.S. Gross Domestic Product (GDP) into imports. U.S. production declines, U.S. jobs and skill pools are destroyed, and the trade deficit increases. Foreign GDP, employment, and exports rise.

U.S. corporations that offshore their production for U.S. markets account for a larger share of the U.S. trade deficit than does the OPEC energy deficit. Half or more of the U.S. trade deficit with China consists of the offshored production of U.S. firms. In 2006, the U.S. trade deficit with China was $233 billion, half of which is $116.5 billion or $10 billion more than the U.S. deficit with OPEC.

The other reason for the dollar's demise is the ignorance and nonchalance of "libertarian free market free trade economists" about offshoring and the trade deficit.

There is a great deal to be said on behalf of free markets and free trade. However, for many economists free trade has become an ideology, and they have ceased to think.

Such economists have become insouciant shills for the offshoring interests that fund their research and institutes. Their interests are tied together with those of the offshoring corporations.

Free trade economists have made three massive errors: (1) they confuse labor arbitrage across international borders with free trade when nothing in fact is being traded, (2) they have forgot the two necessary conditions in order for the classic theory of free trade, which rests on the principle of comparative advantage, to be valid, and (3) they are ignorant of the latest work in trade theory, which shows that free trade theory was never correct even when the conditions on which it is based were prevalent.

When a U.S. firm moves its output abroad, the firm is arbitraging labor (and taxes, regulation, etc.) across international borders in pursuit of absolute advantage, not in pursuit of comparative advantage at home. When the U.S. firm brings its offshored goods and services to the U.S. to be marketed, those goods and services count as imports.

David Ricardo based comparative advantage on two necessary conditions: One is that a country's capital seek comparative advantage at home and not seek absolute advantage abroad. The other is that countries have different relative cost ratios of producing tradable goods. Under the Ricardian conditions, offshoring is prohibited.

Today capital is as internationally mobile as traded goods, and knowledge-based production functions have the same relative cost ratios regardless of the country of location. The famous Ricardian conditions for free trade are not present in today's world.

In the most important development in trade theory in 200 years, the distinguished mathematician Ralph Gomory and the distinguished economist and former president of the American Economics Association, William Baumol, have shown that the case for free trade was invalid even when the Ricardian conditions were present in the world. Their book, *Global Trade and Conflicting National Interests*, first presented as lectures at the London School of Economics, was published in 2000 by MIT Press.

While free trade economists hold on to their doctrine-turned-ideology, the U.S. dollar and the American economy are dying.

One of the great lies of the offshoring interests is that U.S. manufacturing is in trouble because of poor U.S. education and a shortage of U.S. scientists and engineers. Pundits such as Thomas Friedman have helped to spread this ignorance until it has become a dogma. Recently, General Electric CEO Jeffrey Immelt lent his weight to this falsehood. (See "The U.S. No Longer Drives Global Economic Growth," *Manufacturing & Technology News*, Nov. 30, 2007.)

The fact of the matter is that the offshoring of U.S. engineering and R&D jobs and the importation of foreign engineers and scientists on work visas have combined with educational subsidies to produce a surplus of American scientists and engineers, many of whom are unable to find jobs when they graduate from university or become casualties of offshoring and H-1B visas.

Corporate interests continue to lobby Congress for more foreign workers, claiming a non-existent shortage of trained Americans, even as the Commission on Professionals in Science and Technology concludes that real salary growth for American scientists and engineers has been flat or declining for the past ten years. The "long trend of strong U.S. demand for scientific and technical specialists" has come to an end with no signs of revival. (See "Job and Income Growth for Scientists and Engineers Comes to an End," *Manufacturing & Technology News*, November 30, 2007.)

What economist has ever heard of a labor shortage resulting in flat or declining pay?

There is no more of a shortage of U.S. scientists and engineers than there were weapons of mass destruction in Iraq. The U.S. media has no investigative capability and serves up the lies that serve short-term corporate and political interests. If it were not for the Internet that provides Americans with access to foreign news sources, Americans would live in a world of perfect disinformation.

Offshoring interests and economic dogmas have combined to create a false picture of America's economic position. While the ladders of upward mobility are being dismantled, Americans are being told that they have never had it better.

DECEMBER 13, 2007

CHAPTER 19

The Truth About High Oil Prices

HOW TO EXPLAIN THE OIL PRICE? WHY IS IT SO HIGH? ARE WE running out? Are supplies disrupted, or is the high price a reflection of oil company greed or OPEC greed? Are Hugo Chavez and the Saudis conspiring against us? In my opinion, the two biggest factors in oil's high price are the weakness in the U.S. dollar's exchange value and the liquidity that the Federal Reserve is pumping out.

The dollar is weak because of large trade and budget deficits, the closing of which is beyond American political will. As abuse wears out the U.S. dollar's reserve currency role, sellers demand more dollars as a hedge against its declining exchange value and ultimate loss of reserve currency status.

In an effort to forestall a serious recession and further crises in derivative instruments, the Federal Reserve is pouring out liquidity that is financing speculation in oil futures contracts. Hedge funds and investment banks are restoring their impaired capital structures with profits made by speculating in highly leveraged oil future contracts, just as real estate speculators flipping contracts pushed up home prices. The oil futures bubble, too, will pop, hopefully before new derivatives are created on the basis of high oil prices.

There are other factors affecting the price of oil. The prospect of an Israeli/U.S. attack on Iran has increased current demand in order to build stocks against disruption. No one knows the consequence of such an ill conceived act of aggression, and the uncertainty pushes up the price of oil as the entire Middle East could be engulfed in conflagration. However, storage facilities are limited, and the impact on price of larger inventories has a limit.

Saudi Oil Minister Ali al-Naimi recently stated, "There is no justification for the current rise in prices." What the minister means is that there are no shortages or supply disruptions. He means no real reasons as distinct from speculative or psychological reasons.

The run up in oil price coincides with a period of heightened U.S. and Israeli military aggression in the Middle East. However, the biggest jump has been in the last 18 months.

When Bush invaded Iraq in 2003, the average price of oil that year was about $27 per barrel, or about $31 in inflation adjusted 2007 dollars. The price rose another $10 in 2004 to an average annual price of $42 (in 2007 dollars), another $12 in 2005, $7 in 2006, and $4 in 2007 to $65. But in the last few months the price has more than doubled to about $135. It is difficult to explain a $70 jump in price in terms other than speculation.

Oil prices have been high in the past. Until 2008, the record monthly oil price was $104 in December 1979 (measured in December 2007 dollars). As recently as 1998 the real price of oil was lower than in 1946 when the nominal price of oil was $1.63 per barrel. During the Bush regime, the price of oil in 2007 dollars has risen from $27 to approximately $135.

Possibly, the rise in the oil price was held down, prior to the recent jump, by expectations that Democrats would eventually end the conflict and restrain Israel in the interest of Middle East peace and justice for the Palestinians.

Now that Obama has pledged allegiance to AIPAC and adopted Bush's position toward Iran, the high oil price could be a forecast that U.S./Israeli policy is likely to result in substantial supply disruptions. Still, the recent Israeli statements that an attack on Iran was "inevitable" only jumped the oil price about $8.

Perhaps more difficult to understand than the high price of oil are the low U.S. long-term interest rates. U.S. interest rates are actually below the rate of inflation, to say nothing of the imperiled exchange value of the dollar. Economists who assume rational participants in rational markets cannot explain why lenders would indefinitely accept interest rates below the rate of inflation.

Of course, Americans don't get real inflation numbers from their government and have not since the Consumer Price Index was rigged during the Clinton administration to hold down Social Security payments by denying retirees their full cost of living adjustments.

Understating inflation makes real GDP growth appear higher. If inflation were properly measured, the U.S. has probably experienced no real GDP growth in the 21st century.

Statistician John Williams reports that for decades political administrations have fiddled with the inflation and employment numbers to make themselves look slightly better. The cumulative effect has been to deprive these measurements of veracity.

By pumping out money in an effort to forestall recession and paper over balance sheet problems, the Federal Reserve is driving up commodity and food prices in general. Yet American real incomes are not growing. Even without jobs offshoring, U.S. economic policy has put the bulk of the population on a path to lower living standards.

The crisis that looms for the U.S. is the loss of world currency role. Once the dollar loses that role, the U.S. government will not be able to finance its operations by borrowing abroad, and foreigners will cease to finance the massive U.S. trade deficit. This crisis will eliminate the U.S. as a world power.

JUNE 11, 2008

CHAPTER 20

What Uncle Sam has to Tell His Creditors

ACCORDING TO ALL ACCOUNTS THE U.S. FACES ITS WORSE economic crisis since the Great Depression with $2 trillion in near-term financing needs for bailouts and economic stimulus. This is an enormous sum for any country, especially for one that is so heavily indebted that it is close to bankruptcy. If the money can't be borrowed abroad, it will have to be printed—a policy that carries the implication of hyper-inflation.

In normal life a borrower who must appeal to creditors makes every effort to bring order to his financial affairs. But not the Bush regime.

The out-of-pocket costs of Bush's Iraq war are about $600 billion at the present moment, a figure that increases by millions of dollars every hour.

In addition, there are the much larger future costs that have already been incurred, such as long-term care for the wounded and disabled U.S. soldiers, the replacement costs of the used up equipment, interest payments on the war debt, and the lost economic use of the resources and manpower squandered in war. Experts estimate that the already incurred out-of-pocket and future costs of Bush's Iraq war to be $3 trillion and rising.

Even these costs might be small if an article by Richard LaMountain in the November 2008 *Middle American News* is accurate. According to LaMountain, U.S. refugee programs for Iraqis displaced by the U.S. invasion and occupation could result in a large and growing Muslim U.S. population. These would be people whose lives were adversely impacted by the U.S. invasion of Iraq.

If the U.S. maintains its pro-Israeli stance against Arabs and Muslims generally, the implications of a growing Muslim population and a government obsessed with its "war on terror" are frightening for American civil liberty. In order to contain the potential terror that it will have imported, Washington would impose a total police state.

The war must also end in order that bankrupt Washington can borrow abroad the money it needs to bail out the U.S. economy.

The budget authority for the annual out-of-pocket costs of the war have been rising by $150 billion per year, an addition to the budget deficit that must be financed by borrowing abroad. A sane person might think that a government, such as the U.S., in need of foreign loans to save its economy, would jump at the chance to get its troops out of Iraq, where they are not wanted.

Instead the Bush regime has been struggling all year with the Iraq government in order to secure an agreement that lets the U.S. government continue to hemorrhage hundreds of billions of dollars by keeping American troops in Iraq.

The Korean War ended 55 years ago, and the U.S. still has troops in Korea.

Germany was defeated in 1945, and the U.S. still has troops in Germany.

A country that must go hat in hand to its creditors must first look to where costs can be cut. Annual military spending of $700 billion is certainly a good place to start.

But the U.S. government has far more hubris than intelligence and is on its way to being a failed state that has to print money to pay its bills.

It is not too late for the U.S. to save itself and the dollar standard, but it would require a rapid transition from arrogance to humility. The rest of the world can bring America down by not lending to us, in which case neither the trade nor budget deficits could be financed.

The world does not want to bring us down in this way. Our creditors would like to preserve as much as possible the values of their trillions in U.S. dollar assets. This is easier done if the dollar remains the reserve currency. Therefore, the U.S. government has an opportunity to go to its creditors with a plan.

This is what the plan must be: A declaration that repudiates the neo-conservative goal to achieve U.S. hegemony over the world; a budget that reduces annual U.S. borrowing needs by several hundreds of billions by ending the Afghan and Iraq wars, by closing overseas military bases, and by cutting military spending; a new corporate tax system that brings back American jobs, manufacturing capability, and export potential by taxing U.S. corporations' worldwide profits according to the value-added in the U.S.

Such a plan would demonstrate that the U.S. respects the sovereignty and aspirations of other countries and is willing to cooperate peacefully with others as an occupant of what the Russian president has termed "our common house." Such a plan would demonstrate that the U.S. government has come to the realization that there is a limit to its borrowing capacity and the loans that it can service and is prepared to put first things first. Such a plan would show that the U.S. can curtail its unsustainable dependency on imports without erecting a wall of tariffs.

If the U.S. had the leadership to approach its creditors with such a plan, a sigh of relief would emit from the rest of the world. Many of the economic hardships that Americans currently face could be avoided, and the prospect of a hyper-inflationary depression would recede.

Such a favorable outcome requires that the government in Washington give up the delusion that Americans are an "indispensable people" who have a monopoly on virtue that gives them claim to hegemony over the world.

NOVEMBER 20, 2008

CHAPTER 21

America's Third World Service Economy

THE FEBRUARY, 2005, PAYROLL JOBS FIGURES RELEASED LAST FRIDAY by the Bureau of Labor Statistics show a continuation of America's descent into a Third World service economy.

The Bush administration cheered the creation of 229,000 private sector jobs (which still leaves Bush with a net private sector job loss during his reign). However, once we look at the details, the joy vanishes: 174,000 of the jobs, or 76 per cent of the total, are in nontradable services.

Administrative and waste services (largely temporary help and employment services) account for 61,000 or 35 per cent of the new service jobs. The remainder are accounted for by construction (30,000), retail trade (30,000), healthcare and social assistance (27,000), and waitresses and bar-tenders (27,000).

The U.S. has apparently lost the ability to create high productivity, high value-added jobs in tradable goods and services. The ladders of upward mobility are being dismantled by offshore production for home markets and outsourcing of knowledge jobs.

The BLS reports that the number of employed U.S. technical workers has fallen by 221,000 in six major computer and engineering job classifications during 2000–2004. The largest drops were suffered by computer programmers, followed by electrical and electronics engineers, computer scientists, and systems analysts.

So much for the new economy that economists promised would take the place of the lost manufacturing economy.

America's remaining job market is domestic nontradable services. While India and China develop First World job markets, the U.S. labor market takes on the characteristics of a Third World work force. Only jobs that cannot be outsourced are growing.

The Bush economy has seen a loss of 2.8 million manufacturing jobs, a rise in the unemployment rate of 1.2 per centage points, and a stagnation in real weekly earnings.

How bad will things have to get before economists realize that outsourced jobs are not being replaced? Indeed, many American companies are ceasing to have any presence in the U.S. except for a sales force.

Cisco's CEO, John Chambers, declared recently: "What we're trying to do is outline an entire strategy of becoming a Chinese company."

Cisco is establishing a new R&D center in Shanghai. The U.S. corporation manufactures $5 billion of products in China where it employs 10,000 people.

That is just one company, and there are many doing the same thing. The result is abandonment of the American work force by American corporations. Little wonder the Bush administration is the first administration in 70 years to have a net loss of private sector jobs.

If one U.S. company or a few move offshore, their profits improve and consumer prices are lower. However, when work in general moves offshore, American lose the incomes associated with the production of the goods they consume. Domestic production is turned into imports, with the result that America draws down its accumulated wealth in order to pay for the imports on which it is dependent.

The dollar's value and status as reserve currency cannot forever stand the trade and budget deficits that are now part and parcel of America's economic policy.

Unless there are major changes soon, America's economic future is a Third World work force with a banana democracy's worthless currency.

MARCH 10, 2005

CHAPTER 22

China is not the Problem: Offshoring and Free Market Ideology

A T A TIME WHEN EVEN THE *Wall Street Journal* HAS DISAPPEARED into the maw of a huge media conglomerate, the *New York Times* remains an independent newspaper. But it doesn't show any independence in reporting or in thought.

The *Times* issued a mea culpa for letting its reporter, Judith Miller, misinform readers about Iraq, thus helping the neoconservatives set the stage for their invasion. Now the *Times'* reporting on Iran seems to be repeating the mistake. After the U.S. commits another act of naked aggression by bombing Iran, will the *Times* publish another mea culpa?

The *Times'* editorials also serve as conduits for propaganda. On August 13, a *Times* editorial jumped on China for "irresponsible threats" that threaten free trade. The *Times'* editorialists do not understand that the offshoring of American jobs, which the *Times* mistakenly thinks is free trade, is a far greater threat to America than a reminder from the Chinese, who are tired of U.S. bullying, that China is America's banker.

Let's briefly review the "China threat" and then turn to the real problem.

Members of the U.S. government believe, as do many Americans, that the Chinese currency is undervalued relative to the U.S. dollar and that this is the reason for America's large trade deficit with China. Pressure continues to be applied to China to revalue its currency in order to reduce its trade advantage over goods made in the U.S.

The pressure put on China is misdirected. The exchange rate is not the main cause of the U.S. trade deficit with China. The costs of labor, regulation, and harassment are far lower in China, and U.S. corporations have offshored their production to China in order to benefit from these lower costs. When a company shifts its production from the U.S. to a foreign country, it transforms U.S. Gross Domestic Product (GDP) into imports. Every time a U.S. company offshores goods and services, it adds to the U.S. trade deficit.

Clearly, it is a mistake for the U.S. government and economists to think of the imbalance as if it were produced by Chinese companies underselling goods produced by U.S. companies in America. The imbalance is the result of U.S. companies producing their goods in China and selling them in America. Many believe the solution is to force China to revalue its currency, thereby driving up the prices of 70 per cent of the goods on Wal-Mart shelves.

Mysteriously, members of the U.S. government believe that it would help U.S. consumers, who are as dependent on imported manufactured goods as they are on imported energy, to be charged higher prices.

China believes that the exchange rate is not the cause of U.S. offshoring and opposes any rapid change in its currency's value. In a message issued in order to tell the U.S. to ease off the public bullying, China reminded Washington that the U.S. doesn't hold all the cards.

The *New York Times* editorial expresses the concern that China's "threat" will cause protectionist U.S. lawmakers to stick on tariffs and start a trade war. "Free trade, free market" economists rush to tell us how bad this would be for U.S. consumers: A tariff would raise the price of consumer goods.

The free market economists don't tell us that dollar depreciation would have the same effect. Goods made in China would go up 30 per cent in price if a 30 per cent tariff was placed on them, and the goods would go up 30 per cent in price if the value of the Chinese currency rises 30 per cent against the dollar.

So, why all the fuss about tariffs?

The fuss about tariffs makes even less sense once one realizes that the purpose of tariffs is to protect domestically produced goods from cheaper imports. However, U.S. tariffs today would be imposed on the offshored production of U.S. firms. In the era of offshoring, corporations are not a constituency for tariffs.

Tariffs would benefit American labor, something that the U.S. Chamber of Commerce, the National Association of Manufacturers, and the Republican Party would strongly oppose. A wage equalization tariff would wipe out much of the advantage of offshoring. Profits would come down, and with lower profits would come lower CEO compensation and shareholder returns. Obviously, the corporate interests and Wall Street do not want any tariffs.

The *New York Times* and "free trade" economists haven't caught on, because they mistakenly think that offshoring is trade. In fact, offshoring is labor arbitrage. U.S. labor is simply removed from production functions that produce goods and services for U.S. markets and replaced with foreign labor. No trade is involved. Instead of being produced in America, U.S. brand names sold in America are produced in China.

It is not China's fault that American corporations have so little regard for their employees and fellow citizens that they destroy their economic opportunities and give them to foreigners instead.

It is paradoxical that everyone is blaming China for the behavior of American firms. What is China supposed to do, close its borders to foreign capital?

When free market economists align, as they have done, with foreigners against American citizens, they destroy their credibility and the future of economic freedom. Recently the Independent Institute, with which I am associated, stressed that free market associations "have defended completely open immigration and free markets in labor," emphasizing that 500 economists signed the Independent Institute's "Open Letter" on Immigration in behalf of open immigration.

Such a policy is satisfying to some in its ideological purity. But what it means in practice is that the Americans, who are displaced in their professional and manufacturing jobs by offshoring and work visas for foreigners, also cannot find work in the unskilled and semi-skilled jobs taken over by illegal immigrants. A free market policy that gives the bird to American labor is not going to win acceptance by the population. Such a policy serves only the owners of capital and its senior managers.

Free market economists will dispute this conclusion. They claim that offshoring and unrestricted immigration provide consumers with cheaper prices in the market place. What the free market economists do not say is that offshoring and unrestricted immigration also provide U.S. citizens with lower incomes, fewer job opportunities, and less satisfying jobs. There is no evidence that consumer prices fall by more than incomes so that U.S. citizens can be said to benefit materially. The psychological experience of a citizen losing his career to a foreigner is alienating.

The free market economists ignore the fact that a country that off-shores its production also offshores its jobs. It becomes dependent on goods and services made in foreign countries, but lacks sufficient export earnings with which to pay for them. A country whose workforce is being reallocated, under pressure of offshoring, to domestic services has nothing to trade for its imports. That is why the U.S. trade deficit has exploded to over $800 billion annually.

Among all the countries of the world, only the U.S. can get away with exploding trade deficits. The reason is that the U.S. inherited from Great Britain, exhausted by two world wars, the reserve currency role. To be the reserve currency country means that your currency is the accepted means of payment to settle international accounts. Countries pay their oil import bills in dollars and settle the deficits in their trade accounts in dollars.

The enormous and continuing U.S. deficits are wearing out the U.S. dollar as reserve currency. A time will come when the U.S. cannot pay for the imports, on which it has become ever more dependent, by flooding the world with ever more dollars.

Offshoring and free market ideology are turning the U.S. into a Third World country. According to the Bureau of Labor Statistics, one-quarter of all new U.S. jobs created between June 2006 and June 2007 were for waitresses and bartenders. Almost all of the net new U.S. jobs in the 21st century have been in domestic services.

Free market economists simply ignore the facts and proceed with their ideological justifications of open borders, a policy that is rapidly destroying the ladders of upward mobility for the U.S. population.

AUGUST 17, 2007

CHAPTER 23

World Tires of Rule by Dollar

WHAT EXPLAINS THE PARADOX OF THE DOLLAR'S SHARP rise in value against other currencies (except the Japanese yen) despite disproportionate U.S. exposure to the worst financial crisis since the Great Depression?

The answer does not lie in improved fundamentals for the U.S. economy or better prospects for the dollar to retain its reserve currency role.

The rise in the dollar's exchange value is due to two factors.

One factor is the traditional flight to the reserve currency that results from panic. People are simply doing what they have always done. Pam Martens predicted correctly that panic demand for U.S. Treasury bills would boost the U.S. dollar.

The other factor is the unwinding of the carry trade. The carry trade originated in extremely low Japanese interest rates. Investors and speculators borrowed Japanese yen at an interest rate of one-half of one per cent, converted the yen to other currencies, and purchased debt instruments from other countries that pay much higher interest rates. In effect, they were getting practically free funds from Japan to lend to others paying higher interest.

The financial crisis has reversed this process. The toxic American derivatives were marketed worldwide by Wall Street. They have endangered the balance sheets and solvency of financial institutions throughout the world, including national governments, such as Iceland and Hungary. Banks and governments that invested in the troubled American financial instruments found their own debt instruments in jeopardy.

Those who used yen loans to purchase, for example, debt instruments from European banks or Icelandic bonds, faced potentially catastrophic losses. Investors and speculators sold their higher-yielding financial instruments in a scramble for dollars and yen in order to pay off their Japanese loans. This drove up the values of the yen and the U.S. dollar, the reserve currency that can be used to repay debts, and drove down the values of other currencies.

The dollar's rise is temporary, and its prospects are bleak. The U.S. trade deficit will shrink due to less consumer spending during recession, but it will remain the largest in the world and one that the U.S. cannot close by exporting more. The way the U.S. trade deficit is financed is by foreigners acquiring more dollar assets, with which their portfolios are already heavily weighted.

The U.S. government's budget deficit is large and growing, adding hundreds of billions of dollars more to an already large national debt. As investors flee equities into U.S. government bills, the market for U.S. Treasuries will temporarily depend less on foreign governments. Nevertheless, the burden on foreigners and on world savings of having to finance American consumption, the U.S. government's wars and military budget, and the U.S. financial bailout is increasingly resented.

This resentment, combined with the harm done to America's reputation by the financial crisis, has led to numerous calls for a new financial order in which the U.S. plays a substantially lesser role. "Overcoming the financial crisis" are code words for the rest of the world's intent to overthrow U.S. financial hegemony.

Brazil, Russia, India, and China have formed a new group (BRIC) to coordinate their interests.

On October 28, 2008, RIA Novosti reported that Russian prime minister Vladimir Putin suggested to China that the two countries use their own currencies in their bilateral trade, thus avoiding the use of the dollar. China's Prime Minister Wen Jiabao replied that strengthening bilateral relations is strategic.

Europe has also served notice that it intends to exert a new leadership role. Four members of the Group of Seven industrial nations—France, Britain, Germany, and Italy—used the financial crisis to call for sweeping reforms of the world financial system. Jose Manual Barroso, president of the European Commission, said that a new world financial system is possible only "if Europe has a leadership role."

Russian president Dmitry Medvedev said that the "economic egoism" of America's "unipolar vision of the world" is a "dead-end policy."

China's massive foreign exchange reserves and its strong position in manufacturing have given China the leadership role in Asia. The deputy prime minister of Thailand recently designated the Chinese yuan as "the rightful and anointed convertible currency of the world."

Normally, the Chinese are very circumspect in what they say, but on October 24 Reuters reported that the *People's Daily*, the official government newspaper, in a front-page commentary accused the U.S. of plundering "global wealth by exploiting the dollar's dominance." To correct this unacceptable situation, the commentary called for Asian and European countries to "banish the U.S. dollar from their direct trade relations, relying only on their own currencies." And this step, said the commentary, is merely a starting step in overthrowing dollar dominance.

The Chinese are expressing other thoughts that would get the attention of a less deluded and arrogant American government. Zhou Jiangong, editor of the online publication, Chinastates.com, recently asked: "Why should China help the U.S. to issue debt without end in the belief that the national credit of the U.S. can expand without limit?"

Zhou Jiangong's solution to American excesses is for China to take over Wall Street.

China has the money to do it, and the prudent Chinese would do a better job than the crowd of thieves who have destroyed America's financial reputation while exploiting the world in pursuit of multi-million dollar bonuses.

OCTOBER 30, 2008

CHAPTER 24

Supermodel Spurns the Dollar

THE U.S. DOLLAR IS STILL OFFICIALLY THE WORLD'S RESERVE currency, but it cannot purchase the services of Brazilian super model Gisele Bündchen. According to media reports, Gisele required the $30 million she earned during the first half of this year to be paid in euros.

Gisele is not alone in her forecast of the dollar's fate. *The First Post* (U.K.) reports that Jim Rogers, a former partner of billionaire George Soros, is selling his home and all possessions in order to convert all his wealth into Chinese yuan.

Meanwhile, American economists continue to preach that offshoring is good for the U.S. economy and that Bush's war spending is keeping the economy going. The practitioners of supply and demand have yet to figure out that the dollar's supply is sinking the dollar's price and along with it American power.

The macho super patriots who support the Bush regime still haven't caught on that U.S. superpower status rests on the dollar being the reserve currency, not on a military unable to occupy Baghdad. If the dollar were not the world currency, the U.S. would have to earn enough foreign currencies to pay for its 737 oversees bases, an impossibility considering America's $800 billion trade deficit.

When the dollar ceases to be the reserve currency, foreigners will cease to finance the U.S. trade and budget deficits, and the American Empire along with its wars will disappear overnight. Perhaps Bush will be able to get a World Bank loan, or maybe one from the "Chavez bank," to bring the troops home from Iraq and Afghanistan.

Foreign leaders, observing that offshoring and war are accelerating America's relative economic decline, no longer treat the U.S. with the deference to which Washington is accustomed. Ecuador's president, Rafael Correa, recently refused Washington's demand to renew the lease on the

Manta Air Base in Ecuador. He told Washington that the U.S. could have a base in Ecuador if Ecuador could have a military base in the U.S.

When Venezuelan president Hugo Chavez addressed the UN, he crossed himself as he stood at the podium. Referring to President Bush, Chavez said, "Yesterday the devil came here, and it smells of sulfur still today." Bush, said Chavez, was standing "right here, talking as if he owned the world."

In his state of *The Nation* message last year, Russian president Vladimir Putin said that Bush's blathering about democracy was nothing but a cloak for the pursuit of American self-interests at the expense of other peoples. "We are aware what is going on in the world. Comrade wolf knows whom to eat, and he eats without listening, and he's clearly not going to listen to anyone." In May 2007, Putin criticized the neocon regime in Washington for "disrespect for human life" and "claims to global exclusiveness, just as it was in the time of the Third Reich."

Even America's British allies regard President Bush as a threat to world peace and the second most dangerous man alive. Bush is edged out in polls by Osama bin Laden, but is regarded as more dangerous than Iran's demonized president and North Korea's Kim Jong-il.

President Bush has achieved his dismal world standing despite spending $1.6 billion of hard-pressed Americans' tax money on public relations between 2003 and 2006.

Clearly, America's leader and America's currency are poorly regarded. Is there a solution?

Perhaps the answer lies in those 737 overseas bases. If those bases were brought home and shared among the 50 states, each state would gain 15 new military bases. Imagine what this would mean: The end of the housing slump. A reduction in the trade deficit.

And the end of the war on terror.

Who would dare attack a country with 15 new military bases in every state in addition to the existing ones? Wherever a terrorist turned, he would find himself surrounded by soldiers.

All of the dollars currently spent abroad to support 737 overseas bases would be spent at home. Income for foreigners would become income for Americans, and the trade deficit would shrink. The impact of the

737 military base payrolls on the U.S. economy would end the housing crisis and bring back the 140,000 highly paid financial services jobs, the loss of which this year has cost the U.S. $42 billion in consumer income. Foreclosures and bankruptcies would plummet.

If this isn't enough to turn the dollar around, President Bush's pledge not to appoint an Attorney General if Michael Mukasey is not confirmed offers more promise. If the Democrats will defeat Mukasey's nomination, there are other superfluous cabinet departments that can be closed down in addition to the U.S. Department of Torture and Indefinite Detention.

The American empire is being unwound on the battlefields of Iraq and Afghanistan. The year is two months from being over, but already in 2007, despite the touted "surge," deaths of U.S. soldiers are the highest of any year of the war.

The Taliban are the ones who are surging. They have taken control of a third district in western Afghanistan. Turkey and the Kurds are on the verge of turning northern Iraq into a new war zone, another demonstration of American impotence.

Bush's wars have endangered America's puppet regimes. Bush's Pakistani puppet, Musharraf, is fighting for his life. By resorting to "emergency rule" and oppressive measures, Musharraf has intensified his opposition. When Musharraf falls, thanks to Bush, the Islamists will be a step closer to nuclear weapons.

American generals used to say that the wars Bush started in the Middle East would take 10 years to win. On October 31, 2007, General John Abizaid, former commander of U.S. forces in the Middle East, put paid to that optimistic forecast. Speaking at Carnegie Mellon University, Gen. Abizaid said it would be 50 years before U.S. troops can leave the Middle East.

There is no possibility of the U.S. remaining in the Middle East for a half century. The dollar and U.S. power are already on their last legs, unbeknownst to Democratic leaders Pelosi and Reid who are preparing yet another blank check for Bush's latest request for $200 billion in supplementary war funding.

There isn't any money with which to fund Bush's lost war. It will have to be borrowed from China.

The Romans brought on their own demise, but it took them centuries. Bush has finished America in a mere seven years.

Even as Gisele throws off the dollar's hegemony, Brazil, Venezuela, Ecuador, Bolivia, Argentina, Uruguay, Paraguay, and Colombia are declaring independence of the IMF and World Bank, instruments of U.S. financial hegemony, by creating their own development bank, thus bringing to an end U.S. suzerainty over South America.

An empire that has lost its backyard is finished.

NOVEMBER 7, 2007

CHAPTER 25

Farewell to Old Economic Nostrums: They Can't Save Us Now

WITH HIS TAX REBATE POLICY, PRESIDENT BUSH HAS PUT economic policy back on a Keynesian basis. Will it work?

During the two decades it was in effect, supply-side economics had restorative effects on the American economy. Its predecessor, Keynesian demand management, stimulated demand more than supply. Consequently, over time the trade-offs between employment and inflation worsened, and for a while it appeared that inflation and unemployment would rise together. The breakdown of the Keynesian policy opened the door for the Reagan administration's supply-side approach.

By following Nobel economist Robert Mundell's advice to "reverse the policy mix," the supply-side policy allowed the U.S. economy to grow without paying for the growth with rising rates of inflation. However, the new macroeconomic policy was not a cure-all, and its success in banishing worsening "Philips curve" trade-offs between inflation and employment masked the appearance of new problems, such as the loss of jobs and GDP growth to offshoring, problems from deregulation, and the growing concentration of income in fewer hands.

The Bush administration is turning to tax rebates, because problems in the financial system and the amount of consumer debt hinder the Federal Reserve's ability to pump money to consumers through the banking system. Like an easy credit, low interest rate policy, the purpose of a tax rebate is to put money in consumers' hands in order to boost consumer demand.

Will consumers spend the rebate, or will they use it to pay down their debts? If they spend the rebate on consumer goods, will it provide much boost to the economy?

Many Americans are overloaded with debt and will have to use the rebate to pay down credit card debt. The gift of $600 per means-tested taxpayer is really just a partial bailout of heavily indebted consumers and credit card companies.

The per centage of the rebate that survives debt reduction will be further drained of effect by Americans' dependency on imports. According to reports, 70 per cent of the goods on Wal-Mart shelves are made in China. During 2006, Americans spent $1,861,380,000,000 on imported goods, that is, 23 per cent of total personal consumption expenditures were spent on imports (including offshored goods). This means that between one-fifth and one-fourth of new consumption expenditures will stimulate foreign economies.

Americans worry about their dependency on imported energy, but the $145,368,000,000 paid to OPEC in 2006 is a small part of the total import bill. Americans imported $602,539,000,000 in industrial supplies and materials; $418,271,000,000 in capital goods; $256,660,000,000 in automotive vehicles, parts, and engines; $423,973,000,000 in manufactured consumer goods; and $74,937,000,000 in foods, feeds, and beverages.

The Keynesian policy of driving the economy through consumer demand was applied to a different economy than the one we have today. In those days the goods Americans purchased, such as cars and appliances, were mainly made in America. Construction workers were not illegals sending their wages back to Mexico. The U.S. had a robust manufacturing workforce. When consumer demand weakened, companies would reduce their output and lay off workers. Government policymakers would respond to the decline in employment and output with monetary and fiscal policies that boosted consumer demand. As consumer spending picked up, companies would call back the laid off workers in order to increase output to meet the rising demand.

Today Americans are losing jobs for reasons that have nothing to do with recession. They are losing their jobs to offshoring and to foreigners brought in on work visas. Today many American brands are produced offshore in whole or part with foreign labor and imported to the U.S. for sale in the American market. In 2007, prior to the onset of the 2008 recession, 217,000 manufacturing jobs were lost. The U.S. now has fewer manufacturing jobs than it had in 1950 when the population was half the current size.

U.S. job growth in the 21st century has been confined to low-pay domestic services. During 2007, waitresses and bartenders, health care and social assistance, and wholesale and retail trade, transportation, and utilities accounted for 91 per cent of new private sector jobs.

When a population drowning in debt is hit with unemployment from recession on top of unemployment from offshoring, will the people spend their rebates in eating places and bars, thus boosting employment among waitresses and bartenders? Will they spend their rebates in shopping malls, thus boosting employment for retail clerks? If they become ill, the lack of medical insurance will direct their rebates to doctors' bills.

Economists and other shills for globalism told Americans not to worry about the loss of manufacturing jobs. Good riddance, they said, to these "old economy" jobs. The "new economy" would bring better and higher paying jobs in technical and professional services that would free Americans from the drudgery of factory work. So far, these jobs haven't shown up, and if they do, most will be susceptible to offshoring, just like the manufacturing jobs.

The Bush administration has in mind a total rebate of $150,000,000,000. As the government's budget is already in deficit, the money will have to be borrowed. As the U.S. saving rate is about zero, the money will have to be borrowed abroad.

Foreigners are already concerned about the U.S. government's indebtedness, and foreigners are bailing out some of our most important banks and Wall Street firms that foolishly invested in subprime derivatives.

Under pressure from budget and trade deficits, the U.S. dollar has been losing value against other traded currencies. Having to borrow another $150 billion abroad will further erode the dollar's value.

Meanwhile, Congress passed a $700 billion "defense" bill so that the Bush administration can continue its wars in the Middle East.

Our leaders in Washington are out to lunch. They have no idea of the real challenges our country faces and America's dependence on foreign creditors.

The rebate will help Americans reduce their credit card debt. However, adding $150 billion to an existing federal budget deficit that will be worsened by recession could further alarm America's foreign creditors, traders in currency markets, and OPEC oil producers. If the rebate loses its punch to consumer debt reduction, imports, and pressure on the dollar, what will the government do next?

As long as offshoring continues, the U.S. cannot close its trade deficit. Offshoring increases imports and reduces the supply of potential exports. With Washington's Middle East wars, with private companies ceasing to provide health coverage and pensions, with political spending promises in an election year, and with recession, the outlook for the federal budget deficit is dismal as well.

The U.S. is moving into a situation in which the government could find it impossible to close the twin deficits without massive tariffs to curtail imports and offshoring and without pursuing peace instead of war. The outlook for the United States will continue to worsen as long as hegemonic superpower and free trade delusions prevail in Washington.

JANUARY 22, 2008

CHAPTER 26

War Abroad, Poverty at Home

The U.S. Senate has voted $165 billion to fund Bush's wars of aggression against Afghanistan and Iraq through next spring.

As the U.S. is broke and deep in debt, every one of the $165 billion dollars will have to be borrowed. American consumers are also broke and deep in debt. Their zero saving rate means every one of the $165 billion dollars will have to be borrowed from foreigners.

The "world's only superpower" is so broke it can't even finance its own wars.

Each additional dollar that the irresponsible Bush Regime has to solicit from foreigners puts more downward pressure on the dollar's value. During the eight wasted and extravagant years of the Bush Regime, the once mighty U.S. dollar has lost about 40 per cent of its value against the euro.

The dollar has lost even more of its value against gold and oil.

Before Bush began his wars of aggression, oil was $25 a barrel. Today it is $130 a barrel. Some of this rise may result from run-away speculation in the futures market. However, the main cause is the eroding value of the dollar. Oil is real, and unlike paper dollars is limited in supply. With massive U.S. trade and budget deficits, the outpouring of dollar obligations mounts, thus driving down the value of the dollar.

Each time the dollar price of oil rises, the U.S. trade deficit rises, requiring more foreign financing of U.S. energy use. Bush has managed to drive the U.S. oil import bill up from $106 billion in 2006 to approximately $500 billion 18 months later—every dollar of which has to be financed by foreigners.

Without foreign money, the U.S. "superpower" cannot finance its imports or its government's operation.

When the oil price rises, Americans, who are increasingly poor, cannot pay their winter heating bills. Thus, the Senate's military spending bill contains more heating subsidies for America's growing legion of poor people.

The rising price of energy drives up the price of producing and transporting all goods, but American incomes are not rising except for the extremely rich.

The disappearing value of the U.S. dollar, which pushes up oil prices and raises the trade deficit, then pushes up heating subsidies and raises the budget deficit.

If oil was the reason Bush invaded Iraq, the plan obviously backfired. Oil not merely doubled or tripled in price but quintupled.

America's political leaders either have no awareness that Bush's wars are destroying our country's economic position and permanently lowering the living standards of Americans or they do not care. John McCain says he can win the war in Iraq in five more years and in the meantime "challenge" Russia and China. Hillary Clinton says she will "obliterate" Iran. Obama can't make up his mind if he is for war or against it.

The Bush regime's inability to pay the bills it is piling up for Americans means that future U.S. governments will cut promised benefits and further impoverish the people. Over a year ago *The Nation* reported that the Bush regime is shedding veteran costs by attributing consequences of serious war wounds to "personality disorders" in order to deny soldiers promised benefits.

Previous presidents reduced promised Social Security benefits by taxing the benefits (a tax on a tax) and by rigging the cost of living adjustment to understate inflation. Future presidents will have to seize private pensions in order to make minimal Social Security payments.

Currently the desperate Bush regime is trying to cut Medicaid health care for the poor and disabled.

The Republican Party is willing to fund war, but sees everything else as an extravagance. The neoconized war party is destroying the economic prospects of American citizens. Is "war abroad and poverty at home" the Republican campaign slogan for the November election?

MAY 23, 2008

CHAPTER 27

When It's a Clear Day and You Can't See GM

T HE PROSPECTS OF A GOVERNMENT RESCUE FOR THE FOUNDERING American automakers dwindled Thursday as Democratic Congressional leaders conceded that they would face potentially insurmountable Republican opposition," reported the *New York Times* last Friday.

Wow! The entire country is steamed up over the Republicans bailing out a bunch of financial crooks who have paid themselves fortunes in bonuses for destroying America's pensions. Why do Democrats want to protect Republicans from further ignominy by not giving them the opportunity to vote down a bailout for workers? Quick, someone enroll the Democratic Party in Politics 101.

GM's divisions in Canada and Germany are asking those governments for help. It will be something if Canada and Germany come through for the American automaker and the American government doesn't.

Conservative talking heads are saying GM is a "failed business model" unworthy of a $25 billion bailout. These are the same talking heads who favored pouring $700 billion into a failed financial model.

The head of the FDIC is trying to get $25 billion—a measly 3.5 per cent of the $700 billion for the banksters—with which to refinance the mortgages of 2 million of the banksters' victims, and Bush's Secretary of the Treasury Paulson says no. Why aren't the Democrats all over this, too?

Apparently, the Democrats still think they are the minority party or else their aim is to supplant the Republicans as the party of the rich.

Any bailout has its downsides. But if America loses its auto industry, it will lose the suppliers as well and will cease to have a manufacturing sector. For years no-think economists have been writing off America's manufacturing jobs, while deluding themselves and the public with propaganda about a New Economy based on finance.

A country that doesn't make anything doesn't need a financial sector as there is nothing to finance.

The financial crisis has had one good effect. It has cured Democratic economists like Robert Reich and Paul Krugman of their fear of budget deficits. During the Reagan years these two economists saw doom in the "Reagan deficits" despite the fact that OECD data showed that the U.S. at that time had one of the lowest ratios of general government debt to GDP in the industrialized world.

Today Reich and Krugman are unfazed by their recommendations of budget deficits that are many multiples of Reagan's. Moreover, neither economist has given the slightest thought as to how the massive budget deficit that they recommend can be financed.

Both recommend large public spending programs. Krugman puts a price tag of $600 billion on his program. If it takes $700 billion to save the banks and only $600 billion to save the economy, it sounds like a good deal. But this $600 billion is on top of the $700 billion for the banks, the $200 billion for Fannie Mae and Freddie Mac, and the $185 billion for AIG. These figures add to $1.685 trillion, a sum that must be added to the budget deficit due to war and recession (or worse).

What we are talking about here is a minimum budget deficit of $2 trillion. The U.S. has never had to finance a deficit of this magnitude. Where is the money coming from?

The U.S. Treasury doesn't have any money, and neither do Americans, who have lost up to half of their savings and retirement funds and are up to their eyeballs in mortgage and consumer debt. And unemployment is rising.

There are only two sources of financing: foreign creditors and the printing press.

I doubt that foreigners have $2 trillion to lend to the U.S. Thanks to the toxic U.S. financial instruments, they have their own bailouts to finance and economies to stimulate. Moreover, I doubt that foreigners think the U.S. can service a public debt that suddenly jumps by $2 trillion. At 5 per cent interest, the additional debt would add $100 billion to the annual budget deficit. In order to pay interest to creditors, the U.S. would have to borrow more money from them.

Economists and policy-makers are not thinking. This enormous financing need comes not to a well-managed economy that can take the additional debt in its stride. Instead, it comes to an economy so badly managed that there are no reserves.

Massive U.S. trade deficits have been financed by giving up U.S. assets to foreigners, who now own the income flows as well. Budget deficits from years of pointless wars and from unsustainable levels of military spending have helped to flood the world with dollars and to drive down the dollar's exchange value. Consumers themselves are drowning in debt and can provide no lift to the economy. Millions of the best jobs have been moved offshore, and research, design, and innovation have followed them. Considering America's dependency on imports, part of any stimulus package that reaches the consumer will bleed off to foreign countries.

Generally, when countries acquire more debt than they can service, they inflate away the debt. If foreign creditors do not save the Obama administration, the Treasury will print bonds and give them to the Federal Reserve, which will print money by creating checking accounts for the Treasury.

The inflation will be severe, particularly as Americans will not be able to pay for the imports of manufactured goods from abroad on which they have become dependent. The exchange value of the dollar will decline with the domestic inflation. Once inflation is off and running, the printing press dollars will only have goods made in America to chase after. The real crisis has not yet begun.

Paulson should rethink the automakers' and FDIC's proposals. A bank produces nothing but paper. Automakers produce real things that can be sold. Occupied homes are worth more then empty ones.

Paulson's inability to see this is the logical outcome of Wall Street thinking that highly values deals made over pieces of paper at the expense of the real economy.

November 17, 2008

CHAPTER 28

Why the Paulson Plan was a Fraud

I S THE PAULSON BAILOUT ITSELF AS BIG A FRAUD AS THE LEVERAGED subprime mortgages?

There will be more trouble to come if the bailout impairs the U.S. Treasury's credit standing and/or the combination of mark-to-market and short-selling permits short-sellers to prosper by driving more financial institutions into bankruptcy.

A reader's comment and an article by Yale professors Jonathan Koppell and William Goetzmann raise precisely this question of the fraudulence of the Paulson package.

As one reader put it, "We have debt at three different levels: personal household debt, financial sector debt and public debt. The first has swamped the second and now the second is being made to swamp the third. The attitude of our leaders is to do nothing about the first level of debt and to pretend that the third level of debt doesn't matter at all."

The argument for the bailout is that the banks will be free of the troubled instruments and can resume lending and that the U.S. Treasury will recover most of the bailout costs, because only a small per centage of the underlying mortgages are bad. Let's examine this argument.

In actual fact, the Paulson bailout does not address the core problem. It only addresses the problem for the financial institutions that hold the troubled assets. Under the bailout plan, the troubled assets move from the banks' books to the Treasury's. But the underlying problem—the continuing diminishment of mortgage and home values—remains and continues to worsen.

The origin of the crisis is at the homeowner level. Homeowners are defaulting on mortgages. Moving the financial instruments onto the Treasury's books does not stop the rising default rate.

The bailout is focused on the wrong end of the problem. The bailout should be focused on the origin of the problem, the defaulting homeowners. The bailout should indemnify defaulting homeowners and pay off the delinquent mortgages. As Koppell and Goetzmann point out, the financial instruments are troubled because of mortgage defaults. Stopping the problem at its origin would restore the value of the mortgage-based derivatives and put an end to the crisis.

This approach has the further advantage of stopping the slide in housing prices and ending the erosion of local tax bases that result from foreclosures and houses being dumped on the market.

What about the moral hazard of bailing out homeowners who over-leveraged themselves? Ask yourself: How does it differ from the moral hazard of bailing out the financial institutions that over-leveraged themselves, securitized questionable loans, insured them, and sold them as investment grade securities?

Congress should focus the bailout on refinancing the troubled mortgages as the Home Owners' Loan Corp. did in the 1930s, not on the troubled institutions holding the troubled instruments linked to the mortgages. Congress needs to back off, hold hearings, and talk with Koppell and Goetzmann. Congress must know the facts prior to taking action. The last thing Congress needs to do is to be panicked again into agreeing to a disastrous course.

OCTOBER 3, 2008

CHAPTER 29

A Futile Bailout as Darkness Falls on America

MERICA HAS BECOME A PRETTY DISCOURAGING PLACE. Americans, for the most part, will never know what happened to them, because they no longer have a free and responsible press. They have Big Brother's press. For example, on September 28, 2008, a *New York Times* editorial blamed the current financial crisis on "antiregulation disciples of the Reagan Revolution."

What utter nonsense. Every example of deregulation that the *New York Times* editorial provides is located in the Clinton administration and the George W. Bush administration. I was a member of the Reagan administration. We most certainly did not deregulate the financial system.

The repeal of the Glass-Steagall Act, which separated commercial from investment banking, was the achievement of the Democratic Clinton administration. It happened in 1999, over a decade after Reagan left office.

It was in 2000 that derivatives and credit default swaps were excluded from regulation.

The greatest mistake was made in 2004, the year that Reagan died. That year the current Secretary of the Treasury, Henry M. Paulson Jr, was head of the investment bank Goldman Sachs. In the spring of 2004, the investment banks, led by Paulson, met with the Securities and Exchange Commission. At this meeting with the New Deal regulatory agency tasked with regulating the U.S. financial system, Paulson convinced the SEC Commissioners to exempt the investment banks from maintaining reserves to cover losses on investments. The exemption granted by the SEC allowed the investment banks to leverage financial instruments beyond any bounds of prudence.

In place of time-proven standards of prudence, computer models engineered by hot shots determined acceptable risk. As one result Bear

Stearns, for example, pushed its leverage ratio to 33 to 1. For every one dollar in equity, the investment bank had $33 of debt!

It was computer models that led to the failure of Long-Term Capital Management in 1998, the first systemic threat to the financial system. Why the SEC went along with Paulson and set aside capital requirements after the scare of Long-Term Capital Management is inexplicable.

The blame is headed toward SEC chairman Christopher Cox. This is more of Big Brother's disinformation. Cox, like so many others, was a victim of a free market ideology that the market "always knows best."

The 20th century proves that the market is likely to know better than a central planning bureau. It was Soviet Communism that collapsed, not American capitalism. However, the market has to be protected from greed. It was greed, not the market, that was unleashed by deregulation during the Clinton and George W. Bush regimes.

I remember when the deregulation of the financial sector began. One of the first inroads was the legislation, written by bankers, to permit national branch banking. George Champion, former chairman of Chase Manhattan Bank, testified against it. In columns I argued that national branch banking would focus banks away from local business needs.

The deregulation of the financial sector was achieved by the Democratic Clinton administration and by Henry Paulson, Secretary of the Treasury in the George W. Bush administration, with the acquiescence of the Securities and Exchange Commission.

The Paulson bailout saves his firm, Goldman Sachs. The Paulson bailout transfers the troubled financial instruments that the financial sector created from the books of the financial sector to the books of the taxpayers at the U.S. Treasury.

This is all the bailout does. It rescues the guilty.

The Paulson bailout does not address the problem, which is the defaulting home mortgages.

The defaults will continue, because the economy is sinking into recession. Homeowners are losing their jobs, and homeowners are being hit with rising mortgage payments resulting from escalator interest rate clauses in their mortgages that make homeowners unable to service their debt.

Shifting the troubled assets from the financial sectors' books to the taxpayers' books absolves the people who caused the problem from responsibility. As the economy declines and mortgage default rates rise, the U.S. Treasury and the American taxpayers could end up with a $700 billion loss.

Initially, the House, but not the Senate, resisted the bailout of the financial institutions, whose executives had received millions of dollars in bonuses for wrecking the U.S. financial system. However, the people's representatives could not withstand the vague hint of martial law and Great Depression with which Paulson and the Bush administration threatened them. The people's representatives succumbed as they did during the New Deal.

The impotence of Congress traces to the Great Depression. As Theodore Lowi in his classic book, *The End of Liberalism*, makes clear, the New Deal stripped Congress of its law-making power and gave it to the executive agencies. Prior to the New Deal, Congress wrote the laws. After the New Deal, a bill is merely an authorization for executive agencies to create the law through regulations. The Paulson bailout has further diminished the legislative branch's power.

Since Paulson's bailout of his firm and his financial friends does nothing to lessen the default rate on mortgages, how will the bailout play out?

If the $700 billion bailout is based on an estimate of the current amount of bad mortgages, as the recession deepens and Americans lose their jobs, the default rate will rise. The $700 billion might not suffice. The Treasury would have to go hat in hand to its foreign creditors for more loans.

As the U.S. Treasury has not got $7, much less $700 billion, it must borrow the bailout money from foreign creditors, already overloaded with U.S. paper. At what point do America's foreign creditors decide that the additions to U.S. debt exceed what can be repaid?

This question was ignored by the bailout. There were no hearings. No one consulted China, America's principal banker, or the Japanese, or the OPEC sovereign wealth funds, or Europe.

Does the world have a blank check for America's mistakes?

This is the same world that is faced with American demands that countries support with money and lives America's quest for world hegemony. Europeans are dying in Afghanistan for American hegemony. Do Europeans want their banks, which hold U.S. dollars as their reserves, to help Paulson bail out his company and his friends?

The U.S. dollar is the world's reserve currency. It comprises the reserves of foreign central banks. Bush's wars and economic policies are destroying the basis of the U.S. dollar as reserve currency. The day the dollar loses its reserve currency role, the U.S. government cannot pay its bills in its own currency. The result will be a dramatic reduction in U.S. living standards.

Currently Treasuries are boosted by the habitual "flight to quality," but as Treasury debt deepens, will investors still see quality? At what point do America's foreign creditors cease to lend? That is the point at which American power ends. It might be close at hand.

The Paulson bailout is predicated on cleaning up financial institutions' balance sheets and restoring the flow of credit. The assumption is that once lending resumes, the economy will pick up.

This assumption is problematic. The expansion of consumer debt, which kept the economy going in the 21st century, has reached its limit. There are no more credit cards to max out, and no more home equity to refinance and spend. The Paulson bailout might restore trust among financial institutions and enable them to lend to one another, but it doesn't provide a jolt to consumer demand.

Moreover, there may be more shoes to drop. Credit card debt and commercial mortgages could be the next to threaten balance sheets of financial institutions. Apparently, credit card debt has been securitized and sold as well, and not all of the debt is good. In addition, the leasing programs of the car manufacturers have turned sour. As a result of high gasoline prices and absence of growth in take-home pay, the residual values of big trucks and SUVs are less than the leasing programs estimated them to be, thus creating more financial problems.

According to statistician John Williams, who measures inflation, unemployment, and GDP according to the methodology used prior to the Clinton regime's corruption of these measures, real U.S. GDP growth in the 21st century has been negative.

This is not a picture of an economy that a bailout of financial institution balance sheets will revive. As the Paulson bailout does not address the mortgage problem per se, defaults and foreclosures are likely to rise, thus undermining the Treasury's estimate that 90 per cent of the mortgages backing the troubled instruments are good.

Moreover, one consequence of the ongoing financial crisis is financial concentration. It is not inconceivable that the U.S. will end up with a few giant banks.

During the Great Depression of the 1930s, the Home Owners' Loan Corporation (HOLC) refinanced 1 million home mortgages in order to prevent foreclosures. The refinancing apparently succeeded, and HOLC returned a profit. The problem then, as now, was not "deadbeats" who wouldn't pay their mortgages, and the HOLC refinancing did not discourage others from paying their mortgages. Market purists who claim the only solution is for housing prices to fall to prior levels overlook that rising inventories can push prices below prior levels, thus causing more distress. They also overlook the role of interest rates. If a worsening credit crisis dries up mortgage lending and pushes mortgage interest rates higher, the rise in interest rates could offset the fall in home prices, and mortgages would remain unaffordable even in a falling housing market.

Some commentators are blaming the current mortgage problem on the pressure that the U.S. government put on banks to lend to unqualified borrowers. However, whatever breaches of prudence there may have been only affected the earnings of individual institutions. They did not threaten the financial system. The current crisis required more than bad loans. It required securitization and its leverage. It required Fed chairman Alan Greenspan's inappropriate low interest rates, which created a real estate boom. Rapidly rising real estate prices quickly created home equity to justify 100 per cent mortgages. Wall Street analysts pushed financial companies to improve their bottom lines, which they did by extreme leveraging.

An alternative to refinancing troubled mortgages would be to attempt to separate the bad mortgages from the good ones and revalue the mortgage-backed securities accordingly. If there are no further defaults, this approach would not require massive write-offs that threaten the solvency of financial institutions. However, if defaults continue, write-downs would be an ongoing enterprise.

Clearly, all Secretary Paulson thought about was getting troubled assets off the books of financial institutions.

The same reckless leadership that gave us expensive wars based on false premises has now concocted an expensive bailout that addresses the banks' problem, not the economy's.

OCTOBER 6, 2008

CHAPTER 30

Which is Worse: Regulation or Deregulation?

LIBERTARIANS PREACH THE MORALITY OF THE MARKET, AND socialists preach the morality of the state. Those convinced of the market's morality want deregulation; those convinced of the state's morality want regulation.

In truth, neither seems to work.

Consider for example the rules against collusion. The political left imposed this regulatory rule in order to prevent monopoly behavior by companies. One consequence has been that, unable to collude, firms are slaves to their bottom lines. In order to compete successfully in the competitive new world of globalism, firms have curtailed pensions and health insurance for their employees.

Or consider the regulation of new drugs, which drives up costs and delays remedies without, apparently, doing much to improve safety.

Or the fleet mileage standards that regulation imposes on car makers. These regulations destroyed the family station wagon. Families needing carrying capacity turned to vans and to panel trucks. Car makers saw a new market and invented the SUV, which as a "light truck" was exempt from the fleet mileage regulations. The effort to impose fuel economy resulted in cars being replaced by over weight fuel-guzzling SUVs.

On the other hand consider the current troubles resulting from banking and financial deregulation. The losses from this one crisis greatly exceed any gains from deregulation.

Or consider the plight of the de-regulated airlines and deterioration in the quality of air service. Or the higher costs of telephone service and the loss of a blue chip stock for widows and retirement funds that resulted from breaking up AT&T. Or the scandals and uncertainties from utility deregulation, which permits non-energy producers like Enron to contract to deliver electric power.

Economists claim that deregulation results in lower prices. Cheap advanced fare airline ticket prices are cited as evidence. What these economists mean is that the fares without stopovers are cheap to people who can plan their trips in advance. Other passengers subsidize these advanced fares by paying four times as much. Moreover, deregulation has created bottom-line competition that has lowered service, removed meals, and results in periodic bankruptcy, thus forcing the airlines' creditors to pay for the low fares. Pilots, flight attendants, and aircraft maintenance crews subsidize the lower fares with reductions in salaries and pension benefits. Are bankruptcies and mergers leading the industry toward one carrier and the re-emergence of regulation?

Consider the fall-out from trucking deregulation. As in the case of the airlines, the claim was that more communities would be served and costs would decline. But which costs? De-regulation made every minute a bottom-line item. Trucks became bigger, heavier, and travel at higher speeds. Highway safety suffers, and highway maintenance costs rise. The courtesy of truck drivers declined. When trucking was regulated, truckers would stop to help people whose cars had broken down. Today that would throw off the schedule and threaten the bottom-line.

Economists dismiss costs that aren't included in price. For them the cost that matters is the price paid by consumers. The truck that gets there faster delivers cheaper to the consumer. The myriad ways in which people pay the price of deregulation are not part of the price paid at the check-out counter.

Economists also say that offshoring lowers Wal-Mart prices, thus benefitting the consumer. They don't say that by moving jobs abroad offshoring reduces the job opportunities and life-time earnings of the U.S. labor force, or that it wrecks the finances of the laid-off U.S. workers and destroys the tax base of their local communities. None of these costs of offshoring enter into the price of the offshored goods that Americans purchase.

Privatization vs. socialization is another dimension of the conflict. Those who distrust the power of private ownership put faith in public ownership, and those who distrust the power of the state find freedom to be imperiled in the absence of private ownership. Twentieth century experience established that public ownership is economically inefficient without producing offsetting gains in public welfare. Those in charge of nationalized firms live well at the expense of taxpayers and consumers.

Nevertheless, privatization can be pushed too far, and it has. As a result of the upfront cost of building prisons and their high operating costs when in government hands, prisons are being privatized and have become profit-making ventures. Governments avoid the construction costs and contract for incarceration services. Allegedly, the greater efficiency of the private operation lowers the cost.

Private prisons, however, require a constant stream of prisoners. They cannot afford to have vacant cells. If incarceration rates fell, profits would disappear and bankruptcy would descend upon the owners. Thus, privatized prisons create a demand for criminals and, as a result, might actually raise the total cost of incarceration.

The U.S.—the "land of liberty"—has the largest prison population in the world. With 5 per cent of the world's population, the U.S. has 25 per cent of the prison population. The U.S. has 1.3 million more people in prison than crime-ridden Russia, and 700,000 more prisoners than authoritarian China, which has a population four times larger.

In the U.S. the number and kind of crimes have exploded. Prisons are full of drug users, and the U.S. now has "hate crimes" such as the use of constitutionally protected free speech against "protected minorities." It is in the self-interest of prison investors to agitate for yet more criminalization of civil liberties and ordinary human behavior.

The case for deregulation is as ideological as the case for regulation. There is no open-and-shut case for either approach. Such issues should be decided on their merits, but usually are decided by the reigning ideology of an epoch or by powerful interest groups.

The Bush regime has de-regulated the government in the sense that the regime has removed constraints that the Founders put on executive power. This was done in the name of the "war on terror." Simultaneously, Bush has increased the regulation of our travel and communication, spying on our Internet use and specifying to the ounce the quantities of toothpaste and shampoo with which Americans can board commercial airliners.

Crises destroy liberty. Lincoln used the crisis of states withdrawing from the union to destroy states' rights, an essential preservative of liberty in the minds of the Founders. Roosevelt used the Great Depression to destroy the legislative power of Congress by having that power delegated to federal agencies. Bush used 9/11 to assault the civil liberties that protect Americans from a police state.

Perhaps we have now reached a point where both libertarians and left-wingers can agree that the U.S. government desperately needs to be re-regulated and again held accountable to the people.

JANUARY 30, 2008

CHAPTER 31

Deficit Nonchalance

WHO REMEMBERS ECONOMISTS' HYSTERIA OVER THE "REAGAN deficits"? Wall Street was in panic. Reagan's fiscal irresponsibility was bringing the end of the world.

The fiscal year 2009 federal budget deficit that Obama is inheriting, and adding to, will be ten times larger in absolute terms than Reagan's biggest and a much larger share of GDP in per centage terms. Yet, economists are sending up no alarms.

Paul Krugman, for example, couldn't damn Reagan's puny deficits enough. But today he thinks the deficit can't be large enough!

The central issue of the stimulus and bailout plans is how to finance the massive budget deficit. This issue remains unaddressed by economists and policy-makers.

As far as I can tell, the government, its advisers and cheerleaders think financing the deficit will be a cakewalk, like the Iraq War.

I am tempted to claim that economists' nonchalance about the massive deficit is an indication that Krugman and the whole lot of them are converts to supply-side economics—,"deficits don't matter." I triumphed, and economists have become my acolytes. The Nobel Prize will arrive tomorrow.

Only we supply-side economists never said that deficits don't matter. We said that deficits have different causes and consequences. Some are problematic. Some are not, or are less so.

Obama's deficit is problematic. It is a massive deficit, far beyond anything ever before financed on planet Earth. It is arriving at a time when pressures on the dollar as reserve currency have mounted from decades of rising trade deficits. The deficit is hitting the financial markets when the rest of the world is in turmoil from ingestion of toxic Wall Street financial instruments. The U.S. must service massive debt when the U.S. economy is hollowed out from the offshoring of manufacturing and professional service jobs. The Obama deficit is a far more serious deficit than the "Reagan deficits."

As President Reagan's first Assistant Secretary of the Treasury for Economic Policy, my job was to find and implement a cure for "stagflation."

"Stagflation" was the word used to describe the worsening "Phillips curve" trade-offs between inflation and employment. The postwar policy of Keynesian demand management relied on easy money to expand employment and GNP and used recession and unemployment to cool down inflation when inflation got out of hand. Over the years, the trade-offs worsened. It took more inflation to get the economy going, and more unemployment to cool down the inflation.

This problem worsened during Jimmy Carter's presidency. Reagan used the "misery index," the sum of the unemployment and inflation rates, to boot Carter from office.

Keynesian economists concluded from the Great Depression that the way to maintain full employment was for the government to manage aggregate demand. If the sum of consumer and investor demand was not sufficient to maintain full employment, government would step in. By running a deficit in its budget, economists thought that government could add enough additional demand to bring employment up to full.

The way this policy was implemented was to use easy monetary policy to stimulate demand and high tax rates to restrain excessive consumer spending that could push up inflation. The Keynesian economists did not understand that the high tax rates contributed to inflation by restraining the output of goods and services, while the easy money drove up prices.

Keynesians had no solution for the problem their policy had caused, so Congress and President Reagan turned to supply-side economists who offered a solution: restrain demand with tighter monetary policy and increase supply with greater after-tax rewards. Supply-side economics reversed the policy mix of demand-side economists. Instead of easy money and high tax rates, there would be tighter money and lower tax rates.

This change caused consternation. Keynesian economists, who sat atop of the profession, bitterly resented the dethroning of their orthodoxy. They turned on supply-siders with a vengeance. We were "voodoo economists," "trickle-down economists," "tax cuts for the rich economists." Keynesians had been the great defenders of budget deficits, but Reagan's were intolerable. They forgot their own Kennedy tax rate reductions. Supply-siders were bringing the end of the world.

Federal Reserve chairman Paul Volcker was part of the problem. Volcker had limited economic understanding. He did not understand the worsening boom-bust cycle that the Keynesian policy had set the Fed upon. He viewed the Reagan tax rate reductions as a Keynesian stimulus to consumer spending that would worsen the inflation, the subduing of which he saw as his responsibility. He feared that the tax rate reductions would cause inflation and that he would be blamed.

At the Treasury we had weekly meetings with Paul, attempting to bring him into an understanding of what it meant to reverse the policy mix. We patiently explained the importance of the Fed bringing money growth down slowly as the tax rate reductions came into play in order to avoid a monetary shock to the system.

Volcker just couldn't get it. He thought the Reagan Treasury consisted of dangerous inflationists. He went home to the Fed and turned off the money supply, reasoning that if there was no money growth he couldn't be blamed for the inflation that Reagan's fiscal policy would cause.

Volcker's fears were reinforced by his advisors. As the Treasury's representative at the Fed's meeting with its outside advisors, I heard Alan Greenspan, Volcker's successor, tell Paul that in view of the Reagan tax rate reductions (which Greenspan also saw as a demand stimulus) "monetary policy was a weak sister that at best could conduct a rear-guard action."

It was amazing to us at Treasury that the Federal Reserve chairman could not understand that monetary policy controlled inflation and that fiscal policy, or the right kind of fiscal policy, helped control inflation by increasing the output of goods and services.

But this was over Volcker's head. Instead of giving us the gradual reduction in the growth of the money supply, he slammed on the brakes.

The economy went into a serious recession just as Reagan's tax cuts passed.

The embittered Keynesians wanted to blame the recession on the tax cuts, but that was inconsistent with their own analysis. So they seized on the deficits that resulted from the recession and blamed the tax cuts. This was also inconsistent with Keynesian analysis. However, they used writings by people who had popularized supply-side economics. Some of these people made claims that "tax cuts pay for themselves." In other words, there would be no deficits.

No supply-side economist ever said this. And neither did the Reagan administration. The Reagan administration used static tax analysis and forecast that every dollar of tax cut would lose a dollar of revenue.

The forecast went wrong for an entirely different reason. The Keynesian orthodoxy of the time was that it was impossible for the economy to grow without paying for it with a rising rate of inflation. Yet, the supply-side position was that by reversing the policy mix, the economy could grow while the rate of inflation fell, which is in fact what happened during the 1980s and 1990s.

As economic forecasting was locked into the "Phillips curve"—the belief that inflation was the price of full employment and that unemployment was the price of lower inflation—the Reagan administration's budget forecast was restrained by the "Phillips curve." Orthodoxy would not permit us to forecast the extent to which a supply-side policy would bring down inflation as the economy grew. Even if we had been able to disregard forecasting orthodoxy, our forecast would have been off as Volcker brought money growth in below target.

The "Reagan deficits" thus resulted from the unanticipated collapse of inflation. As inflation came in below forecast, nominal GNP came in below forecast. Thus, tax revenues were less. But appropriation bills are in nominal dollars, which meant that real spending was greater than intended because inflation was less than forecast.

Wall Street believed that the "Reagan deficits" would cause inflation, but, of course, they did not cause inflation as they were the consequences of the collapse in inflation.

This shows how totally wrong conventional opinion can be even when it tries to think. Today no policy-maker or establishment economist is thinking at all.

The "Reagan deficits" were not financed by printing money or dependent on recycling of surplus dollars by trading partners. The deficits were no threat to the dollar, which was thought to be too strong. The increased after-tax return on investment reduced the flow of U.S. capital abroad, and we financed our own deficit.

This brings us back to the original question: How is the Obama deficit going to be financed?

FEBRUARY 13, 2009

CHAPTER 32

Is It Time to Bail Out of America?

ALIFORNIA STATE CONTROLLER JOHN CHIANG ANNOUNCED ON January 26, 2009, that California's bills exceed its tax revenues and credit line and that the state is going to print its own money known as IOUs. The template is already designed.

Instead of receiving their state tax refunds in dollars, California residents will receive IOUs. Student aid and payments to disabled and needy will also come in the form of IOUs. California is negotiating with banks to get them to accept the IOUs as deposits.

California is often identified as the world's eighth largest economy, and it is broke.

A person might think that California's plight would introduce some realism into Washington, D.C., but it has not. President Obama is taking steps to intensify the war in Afghanistan and to expand it to Pakistan.

Obama has retained the Republican warmongers in the Pentagon, and the U.S. continues to illegally bomb Pakistan and to murder its civilians. At the World Economic Forum at Davos this week, Pakistan's prime minister, Y. R. Gilani, said that the American attacks on Pakistan are counterproductive and done without Pakistan's permission. In an interview with CNN, Gilani said: "I want to put on record that we do not have any agreement between the government of the United States and the government of Pakistan."

How long before Washington will be printing money?

On January 28, Obama announced his $825 billion economic stimulus plan. This comes on top of President Bush's $700 billion bank bailout of just a few months ago.

Obama says his plan will be more transparent than Bush's and will do more good for the economy.

As large as the bailouts are—a total of $1.5 trillion in four months—the amount is small in relation to the reported size of troubled assets that are in the tens of trillions of dollars. How do we know that there won't be another bailout, say $950 billion?

Where will the money come from?

Obama's bailout plan, added to the FY 2009 budget deficit he has inherited from Bush, opens a gaping expenditure hole. Who is going to fill the gap with their savings?

Not the U.S. consumer. The consumer is out of work and out of money. Private sector credit market debt is 174 per cent of GDP. The personal savings rate is 2 per cent. Ten per cent of households are in foreclosure or arrears. Household debt-service ratio is at an all-time high. Household net worth has declined at a record rate. Housing inventories are at record highs.

Not America's foreign creditors. At best, the Chinese, Japanese, and Saudis can recycle their trade surpluses with the U.S. into Treasury bonds, but the combined surplus does not approach the size of the U.S. budget deficit.

Perhaps another drop in the stock market will drive Americans' remaining wealth into "safe" U.S. Treasury bonds.

If not, there's only the printing press.

The printing press would turn a deflationary depression into an inflationary depression. Unemployment combined with rising prices would be a killer.

Inflation would kill the dollar as well, leaving the U.S. unable to pay for its imports.

All the Obama regime sees is a "credit problem." But the crisis goes far beyond banks' bad investments. The United States is busted. Many of the state governments are busted. Homeowners are busted. Consumers are busted. Jobs are busted. Companies are busted.

And Obama thinks he has the money to fight wars in Afghanistan and Pakistan.

Except for the super-rich and those banksters and CEOs who stole wealth from investors and shareholders, Americans have suffered enormous losses in wealth and income.

The stock market decline has destroyed about 45 per cent of their IRAs, 401Ks, and other equity investments. On top of this comes the decline in home prices, lost jobs and health care, lost customers. The realized gains in mutual funds and investment partnerships, on which Americans paid taxes, have been wiped out.

The government should give those taxes back.

Americans who have seen their retirement savings devastated by complicity of government regulators and lawmakers with financial gangsters should not have to pay any income tax when they draw on their pensions.

The financial damage inflicted on Americans by their own government is as great as would be expected from foreign conquest. While Washington "protected" us from terrorists by fighting pointless wars abroad, the U.S. economy collapsed.

How can President Obama even think about fighting wars half way around the world while California cannot pay its bills, while Americans are being turned out of their homes, while, as *Business Week* reports, retirees will work throughout their retirement (which assumes that there will be jobs), while careers are being destroyed and stores and factories shuttered?

Americans are facing tremendous unemployment and hardship. Obama doesn't have another dollar to spend on Bush's wars.

Taxpayers are busted. They cannot stand another day of being milked by the military-security complex. The U.S. government is paying private mercenaries more by the day than the monthly checks it is providing to Social Security retirees.

This is insanity.

The banksters robbed us twice. First it was our home and stock values. Then the government rewarded the banksters for their misdeeds by bailing out the banksters, not their victims, and putting the cost on the taxpayers' books.

The government has also robbed the taxpayers of $3 trillion to fight its wars.

When foreign creditors look at the debt piled on the taxpayers' books, they don't see a good credit risk.

Washington is so accustomed to ripping off the taxpayers for the benefit of special interests that the practice is now in the DNA. While bailouts are being piled upon bailouts, wars are being piled upon wars.

Before Obama gets in any deeper, he must ask his economic team where the money is coming from. When he finds out, he needs to tell the rest of us.

JANUARY 29, 2009

CHAPTER 33

Was the Bailout a Scam?

P ROFESSOR MICHAEL HUDSON (*CounterPunch*, MARCH 18, 2009) is correct that the orchestrated outrage over the $165 million AIG bonuses is a diversion from the thousand times greater theft from taxpayers of the approximately $185 billion "bailout" of AIG. Nevertheless, it is a diversion that serves an important purpose. It has taught an inattentive American public that the elites run the government in their own private interests.

Americans are angry that AIG executives are paying themselves millions of dollars in bonuses after having cost the taxpayers an exorbitant sum. Senator Charles Grassley put a proper face on the anger when he suggested that the AIG executives "follow the Japanese example and resign or go commit suicide."

Yet, Obama's White House economist, Larry Summers, on whose watch as Treasury Secretary in the Clinton administration financial deregulation got out of control, invoked the "sanctity of contracts" in defense of the AIG bonuses.

But the Obama administration does not regard other contracts as sacred. Specifically: labor unions had to agree to give-backs in order for the auto companies to obtain federal help; CNN reports that "Veterans Affairs Secretary Eric Shinseki confirmed Tuesday [March 10] that the Obama administration is considering a controversial plan to make veterans pay for treatment of service-related injuries with private insurance;" the *Washington Post* reports that the Obama team has set its sights on downsizing Social Security and Medicare.

According to the *Post*, Obama said that "it is impossible to separate the country's financial ills from the long-term need to rein in health-care costs, stabilize Social Security and prevent the Medicare program from bankrupting the government."

After Washington's trillion dollar bank bailouts and trillion dollar gratuitous wars for the sake of the military industry's profits and Israeli territorial expansion, there is no money for Social Security and Medicare. It is the payroll tax-supported programs on which ordinary Americans depend that are blamed for bankrupting the government, not the trillions of dollars squandered in pointless wars and bailouts of banksters.

The U.S. government breaks its contracts with U.S. citizens on a daily basis, but AIG's bonus contracts are sacrosanct. The Social Security contract was broken when the government decided to tax 85 per cent of the benefits. It was broken again when the Clinton administration rigged the inflation measure in order to beat retirees out of their cost-of-living adjustments. To have any real Medicare coverage, a person has to give up part of his Social Security check to pay Medicare Part B premium and then take out a private supplemental policy. The true cost of full coverage to Medicare beneficiaries is about $6,000 annually in premiums, plus deductibles and the Medicare tax if the person is still earning.

Treasury Secretary Timothy Geithner, the fox in charge of the hen house, has resolved the problem for us. He is going to withhold $165 million (the amount of the AIG bonuses) from the next taxpayer payment to AIG of $30 billion. If someone handed you $30,000 dollars, would you mind if they held back $165?

PR flaks have rechristened the bonus payments "retention payments" necessary if AIG is to retain crucial employees. This lie was shot down by New York Attorney General Andrew Cuomo, who informed the House Committee on Financial Services that the payments went to members of AIG's Financial Products subsidiary, "the unit of AIG that was principally responsible for the firm's meltdown." As for retention, Cuomo pointed out that "numerous individuals who received large 'retention' bonuses are no longer at the firm."

Eliot Spitzer, the former New York governor who was setup in a sex scandal to prevent him investigating Wall Street's financial gangsterism, pointed out on March 17 that the real scandal is the billions of taxpayer dollars paid to the counter-parties of AIG's financial deals. These payments, Spitzer writes, are "a way to hide an enormous second round of cash to the same group that had received TARP money already."

Goldman Sachs, for example, had already received a taxpayer cash infusion of $25 billion and was sitting on more than $100 billion in cash when the Wall Street firm received another $13 billion via the AIG bailout.

Moreover, in my opinion, most of the billions of dollars in AIG counter-party payments were unnecessary. They represent gravy paid to firms that had made risk-free bets, the non-payment of which constituted no threat to financial solvency.

Spitzer identifies a conflict of interest that could possibly be criminal self-dealing. According to reports, the AIG bailout decision involved Bush Treasury Secretary Henry Paulson, formerly of Goldman Sachs, Goldman Sachs CEO Lloyd Blankfein, Fed Chairman Ben Bernanke, and Timothy Geithner, former New York Federal Reserve president and currently Secretary of the Treasury. No doubt the incestuous relationships are the reason the original bailout deal had no oversight or transparency.

The Bush/Obama bailouts require serious investigation. Were these bailouts necessary, or were they a scam, like "weapons of mass destruction," used to advance a private agenda behind a wall of fear? Recently I heard Harvard Law professor Elizabeth Warren, a member of a congressional bailout oversight panel, say on NPR that the U.S. has far too many banks. Out of the financial crisis, she said, should come consolidation with the financial sector consisting of a few mega-banks. Was the whole point of the bailout to supply taxpayer money for a program of financial concentration?

MARCH 19, 2009

CHAPTER 34

President of Special Interests

T HE BUSH/OBAMA BAILOUT/STIMULUS PLANS ARE NOT GOING TO work. Both are schemes hatched by a clique of financial insiders. The schemes will redistribute income and wealth from American taxpayers to the shyster banksters, who have destroyed American jobs, ruined the retirement plans of tens of millions of Americans, and worsened the situation of millions of people worldwide who naively trusted American financial institutions. The ongoing theft has simply been recast. Instead of using fraudulent financial instruments, the banksters are using government policy.

Michael Hudson captures the nature of the heist in *CounterPunch*, February 12, 2009:

> When it comes to cleaning up the Greenspan Bubble legacy by writing down homeowner mortgage debt, the Treasury proposal offers homeowners $50 billion—just [half of one per cent] of the $10 trillion Wall Street bailout to date, and less than half the amount given to AIG to pay its hedge fund speculators on their derivative gambles. The Treasury has handed out $25 billion to each and every big bank, so just two of these banks alone got as much as the reported one-quarter of all homeowners in America suffering from Negative Equity on their homes and in need of mortgage renegotiation. Yet today's economic shrinkage cannot be reversed without a recovery in consumer demand. The economy has lost the 'virtual wealth' in higher-priced homes and the stock market, and must rely on after-tax earnings. But I see little concern for wage earners in the Treasury plan. Without debt relief, consumer spending and business investment will not recover.

The big money men cannot conceive of anyone's suffering except the mega-rich. If billions are not at stake, what is the problem? How can families losing their homes bring down the economy?

There was a time in America when the interests of elites were connected to those of ordinary Americans. Henry Ford said that he paid his workers good wages so they could buy his cars.

Today American corporations pay foreign workers low wages so CEOs can pay themselves multi-million dollar "performance" bonuses.

Congress has had a parade of CEOs, ranging from Bill Gates of Microsoft and IBM brass on down the line, to testify that they desperately need more H-1B work visas for foreign employees as they cannot find enough American software engineers and IT workers to grow their businesses. Yet, all the companies who sing this song have established records of replacing American employees with H-1B workers who are paid less.

Just the other day Microsoft, IBM, Texas Instruments, Sprint-Nextel, Intel, Motorola, and scores of other corporations announced thousands of layoffs of the qualified American engineers who "are in short supply."

IBM has offered to help to relocate its "redundant" but "scarce" American engineers to its operations in India, China, Brazil, Mexico, the Czech Republic, Russia, South Africa, Nigeria, and the United Arab Emirates at the salaries prevailing in those countries.

On January 28, *USA Today* reported: "In 2007, the last full year for which detailed employment numbers are available, 121,000 of IBM's 387,000 workers [31 per cent] were in the U.S. Meanwhile, staffing in India has jumped from just 9,000 workers in 2003 to 74,000 workers in 2007."

In order to penetrate and to serve foreign markets, U.S. corporations need overseas operations. There is nothing unusual or unpatriotic about this. However, many U.S. companies use foreign labor to manufacture abroad the products that they sell in American markets. If Henry Ford had used Indian, Chinese, or Mexican workers to manufacture his cars, Indians, Chinese, and Mexicans could possibly have purchased Fords, but not Americans.

Senators Charles Grassley and Bernie Sanders offered an amendment to the Troubled Asset Relief Program (TARP) bill that would prevent companies receiving bailout money from discharging American employees and replacing them with foreigners on H-1B visas.

The U.S. Chamber of Commerce, no longer an American institution, and immigration advocates, such as the American Immigration Lawyers Association, immediately went to work to defeat or to water down the amendments. Senator Grassley's attempt to prevent American corporations from replacing American workers with foreigners on H-1B work visas in the midst of the most serious economic crisis since the Great Depression was met with outrage from the U.S. Chamber of Commerce, an organization concerned solely with the multi-million dollar bonuses paid to American CEOs for reducing labor costs by offshoring American jobs or by replacing American employees with foreign guest workers.

On January 23, Senator Grassley wrote to Microsoft CEO Steve Ballmer:

> I am concerned that Microsoft will be retaining foreign guest workers rather than similarly qualified American employees when it implements its layoff plan. As you know, I want to make sure employers recruit qualified American workers first before hiring foreign guest workers. For example, I cosponsored legislation to overhaul the H-1B and L-1 visa programs to give priority to American workers and to crack down on unscrupulous employers who deprive qualified Americans of high-skilled jobs. Fraud and abuse is rampant in these programs, and we need more transparency to protect the integrity of our immigration system.
>
> Last year, Microsoft was here on Capitol Hill advocating for more H-1B visas. The purpose of the H-1B visa program is to assist companies in their employment needs where there is not a sufficient American workforce to meet their technology expertise requirements. However, H-1B and other work visa programs were never intended to replace qualified American workers. Certainly, these work visa programs were never intended to allow a company to retain foreign guest workers rather than similarly qualified American workers, when that company cuts jobs during an economic downturn. It is imperative that in implementing its layoff plan, Microsoft ensures that American workers have priority in keeping their jobs over foreign workers on visa programs.
>
> My point is that during a layoff, companies should not be retaining H-1B or other work visa program employees over qualified American workers. Our immigration policy is not intended to harm the American workforce. I encourage Microsoft to ensure that Americans are given priority in job retention. Microsoft has a moral obligation to protect these American workers by putting them first during these difficult economic times.

Senator Grassley is rightly concerned that recession layoffs will shield increased jobs offshoring and use of H-1B workers. On February 13, the Russian newspaper *Pravda* reported that "America has begun the initial steps to final outsourcing of its last dominant industry"—oil/gas and oil/gas services. *Pravda* reports that "as with other formerly dominant industries, such as light manufacturing, IT, textiles," recession is "used as the knife to finally do in the workers."

According to *Pravda*:

> It is a prime example. The companies used the bust to lay off hundreds of thousands of tech workers around the U.S. and Britain, citing low profits or debt. The public as a whole accepted this, as part of the economic landscape and protests were few, especially with a prospect of the situation turning around. However, shortly after the turn around in the economy, it became very clear that there would be no turn around in the IT employment industry. Not only were companies outsourcing everything they could, under the cover of the recession, they had shipped in tens of thousands of H-1B work visaed workers who were paid on the cheap.

It is rare to find U.S. representatives and senators, such as Grassley, who will take a stand against powerful special interests. Some do so inadvertently, forgetting that patriotism is no longer a characteristic of the American business elite. Hoping to stimulate American rather than foreign businesses, the House version of the economic stimulus bill, the American Recovery and Reinvestment Act of 2009, required that funds provided by the bill cannot be used to purchase foreign-made iron, steel, and textiles.

The Senate provision was more sweeping, mandating that all manufactured goods purchased with stimulus money be American-made.

The U.S. Chamber of Commerce, the National Association of Manufacturers, Caterpillar, General Electric, other transnational corporations, and editorial writers whose newspapers are dependent on corporate advertising set out to defeat the buy American requirement. As far as these anti-American organizations are concerned, the stimulus bill has nothing to do with American jobs or the American economy. It only has to do with the special interest appetites that have the political power to rip off the American taxpayers (see *Manufacturing & Technology News*, February 4, 2009).

Senator John McCain is their man. "Protectionism" exclaimed the man the Republicans wanted as president. McCain said the buy American provision would cause a second Great Depression. U.S. Chamber of Commerce President Thomas Donohue said that buying abroad was "economic patriotism."

The American economic elite are hiding their treason to the American people behind "free trade."

I want to say this as clearly as it can be said. The offshoring of American jobs is the antithesis of free trade. Free trade is based on comparative advantage. Jobs offshoring is an activity in pursuit of lowest factor cost—an activity that David Ricardo, the originator of the free trade theory, described as the betrayal of one's own country in pursuit of "absolute advantage."

The "free market" shills on the payroll of the U.S. Chamber, N.A.M., and in economics departments and think tanks that are recipients of grants from transnational corporations are whores aligned with elites who are destroying the American work force.

Obama has appointed to his National Economic Council blatant apologists for the offshoring of American jobs.

Possibly Obama loves the country that elevated him to its highest office. But his administration is populated with people whose loyalty is limited to elites.

FEBRUARY 18, 2009

CHAPTER 35

Driving Over the Cliff
With the Washington Morons

I S THERE INTELLIGENT LIFE IN WASHINGTON, D.C.? NOT A SPECK OF it.

The U.S. economy is imploding, and Obama is being led into a quagmire in Afghanistan that could bring the U.S. into confrontation with Russia and China, American's largest creditor.

The January, 2009 payroll job figures reveal that last month 20,000 Americans lost their jobs every day.

In addition, December's job losses were revised up by 53,000 jobs from 524,000 to 577,000. The revision brings the two-month job loss to 1,175,000. If this keeps up, Obama's promised 3 million new jobs will be wiped out by job losses.

Statistician John Williams reports that this huge number is an understatement. Williams notes that built-in biases in seasonal adjustment factors caused a 118,000 understatement of January job losses, bringing the actual January job loss to 716,000 jobs.

The payroll survey counts the number of jobs, not the number of employed as some people have more than one job. The Household Survey counts the number of people who have jobs. The Household Survey shows that 832,000 people lost their jobs in January and 806,000 in December, for a two month reduction of Americans with jobs of 1,638,000.

The unemployment rate reported in the U.S. media is a fabrication. Williams reports that since the Clinton era, "'discouraged workers'— those who had given up looking for a job because there were no jobs to be had—were redefined so as to be counted only if they had been 'discouraged' for less than a year. This time qualification defined away the bulk of the discouraged workers. Adding them back into the total unemployed, actual unemployment, (according to the unemployment rate methodology used in 1980) rose to 18 per cent in January, from 17.5 per cent in December."

In other words, without all the manipulations of the data, the U.S. unemployment rate in January 2009 is already at depression levels.

How could it be otherwise given the enormous job loss from off-shored jobs? It is impossible for a country to create jobs when its corporations are moving production for the American consumer market off-shore. When they move the production offshore, they shift U.S. GDP to other countries. The U.S. trade deficit over the past decade has reduced U.S. GDP by $1.5 trillion. That is a lot of jobs.

I have been reporting for years that university graduates have had to take jobs as waitresses and bartenders. As over-indebted consumers lose their jobs, they will visit restaurants and bars less frequently. Consequently, those with university degrees will not even have jobs waiting on tables and mixing drinks.

U.S. policymakers have ignored the fact that consumer demand in the 21st century has been driven, not by increases in real income, but by increased consumer indebtedness. This fact makes it pointless to try to stimulate the economy by bailing out banks so that they can lend more to consumers. The American consumers have no more capacity to borrow.

With the decline in the values of their principal assets—their homes—with the destruction of half of their pension assets, and with joblessness facing them, Americans cannot and will not spend.

Why bail out GM, Citibank, and the rest when the firms are worsening U.S. unemployment by moving as many operations offshore as they possibly can?

Much of U.S. infrastructure is in poor shape and needs renewing. However, infrastructure jobs do not produce goods and services that can be sold abroad. Obama's stimulus commitment to infrastructure does nothing to help the U.S. reduce its huge trade deficit, the financing of which is becoming a major problem. Moreover, when the infrastructure projects are completed, so are the jobs.

At best, assuming Mexican immigrants do not get most of the construction jobs, all Obama's stimulus program can do is to reduce the number of unemployed temporarily.

Unless U.S. corporations can be required to use American labor to produce the goods and services that they sell in American markets, there is no hope for the U.S. economy. No one in the Obama administration has the wits to address this problem. Thus, the economy will continue to implode.

Adding to the brewing disaster, Obama has been deceived by his military and neoconservative advisers into expanding the war in Afghanistan. Obama intends to use the draw-down of U.S. soldiers in Iraq to send 30,000 more American troops to Afghanistan. This would bring the U.S. forces to 60,000—600,000 fewer than U.S. Marine Corps and U.S. Army counterinsurgency guidelines define as the minimum number of soldiers necessary to bring success in Afghanistan.

In Iraq, the Iranian government had to bail out the Bush regime by restraining its Shi'ite allies and encouraging them to use the ballot box to attain power and push out the Americans. In Iraq the U.S. troops only had to fight a small Sunni insurgency drawn from a minority of the population. Even so, the U.S. "prevailed" by putting the insurgents on the U.S. payroll and paying them not to fight. The withdrawal agreement was dictated by the Shi'ites. It was not what the Bush regime wanted.

One would think that the experience with the "cakewalk" in Iraq would make the U.S. hesitant to attempt to occupy Afghanistan, an undertaking that would require the U.S. to occupy parts of Pakistan. The U.S. was hard pressed to maintain 150,000 troops in Iraq. Where is Obama going to get another half million soldiers to add to the 150,000 to pacify Afghanistan?

One answer is the rapidly growing massive U.S. unemployment. Americans will sign up to go kill abroad rather than be homeless and hungry at home.

But this solves only half of the problem. Where does the money come from to support an army in the field of 650,000, an army 4.3 times larger than U.S. forces in Iraq, a war that has cost us $3 trillion in out-of-pocket and already-incurred future costs. This money would have to be raised in addition to the $2 trillion U.S. budget deficit that is the result of Bush's financial sector bailout, Obama's stimulus package, and the rapidly failing economy. When economies tank, as the American one is doing, tax revenues collapse. The millions of unemployed Americans are not paying Social Security, Medicare, and income taxes. The stores and businesses that are closing are not paying federal and state income taxes. Consumers with no money or credit to spend are not paying sales taxes.

The Washington Morons, and morons they are, have given no thought as to how they are going to finance fiscal year 2009 and fiscal year 2010 budget deficits, each of which is four times larger than the 2008 deficit.

The practically nonexistent U.S. saving rate cannot finance it.

The trade surpluses of our trading partners, such as China, Japan, and Saudi Arabia, cannot finance it.

The U.S. government really has only two possibilities for financing such stupendous budget deficits. One is a second collapse in the stock market, which would drive the surviving investors with what they have left into "safe" U.S. Treasury bonds. The other is for the Federal Reserve to monetize the Treasury debt.

Monetizing the debt means that when no one is willing or able to purchase the Treasury's bonds, the Federal Reserve buys them by creating bank deposits for the Treasury's account.

In other words, the Fed "prints money" with which to buy the Treasury's bonds. The Treasury pays the U.S. government's bills by writing checks against the printed money.

Once this happens, the U.S. dollar will cease to be the reserve currency.

China, Japan, and Saudi Arabia, countries that hold enormous quantities of U.S. Treasury debt in addition to other U.S. dollar assets, will sell, hoping to get out before others.

The value of the U.S. dollar will collapse and become the currency of a banana republic.

The U.S. will not be able to pay for its imports, a serious problem for a country dependent on imports for its energy, manufactured goods, and advanced technology products.

Obama's Keynesian advisers have learned with a vengeance Milton Friedman's lesson that the Great Depression resulted from the Federal Reserve permitting a contraction of the supply of money and credit. In the Great Depression good debts were destroyed by monetary contraction. Today bad debts are being preserved by the expansion of bank reserves, and the U.S. Treasury is jeopardizing its credit standing and the dollar's reserve currency status with enormous quarterly bond auctions as far as the eye can see.

Meanwhile, the Russians, overflowing with energy and mineral resources, and not in debt, have learned that the U.S. government is not to be trusted. Russia has watched Reagan's successors attempt to turn former constituent parts of the Soviet Union into U.S. puppet states with U.S. military bases. The U.S. is trying to ring Russia with missiles that neutralize Russia's strategic deterrent.

Putin has caught on to "comrade wolf." To stop America's meddling in Russia's sphere of influence, the Russian government has created a collective security treaty organization comprised of Russia, Armenia, Belarus, Kazakhstan, Kyrgyzstan, and Tajikistan. Uzbekistan is a partial participant.

To whose agenda is President Obama being hitched? Writing in the English language version of the Swiss newspaper, *Zeit-Fragen*, Stephen J. Sniegoski reports that leading figures of the neocon conspiracy— Richard Perle, Max Boot, David Brooks, and Mona Charen—are ecstatic over Obama's appointments. They don't see any difference between Obama and Bush/Cheney.

Not only are Obama's appointments moving him into an expanded war in Afghanistan, but the powerful Israel Lobby is pushing Obama toward a war with Iran.

The unreality in which he U.S. government operates is beyond belief. A bankrupt government that cannot pay its bills without printing money is rushing headlong into wars in Afghanistan, Pakistan, and Iran. According to the Center for Strategic and Budgetary Analysis, the cost to the U.S. taxpayers of sending a single soldier to fight in Afghanistan or Iraq is $775,000 per year!

Obama's war in Afghanistan is the Mad Hatter's Tea Party. After seven years of conflict, there is still no defined mission or endgame scenario for U.S. forces in Afghanistan. When asked about the mission, a U.S. military official told NBC News, "Frankly, we don't have one." NBC reports: "They're working on it."

Speaking to House Democrats on February 5, President Obama admitted that the U.S. government does not know what its mission is in Afghanistan and that to avoid "mission creep without clear parameters," the U.S. "needs a clear mission."

How would you like to be sent to a war, the point of which no one knows, including the commander-in-chief who sent you to kill or be killed? How, fellow taxpayers, do you like paying the enormous cost of sending soldiers on an undefined mission while the economy collapses and your job disappears?

FEBRUARY 9, 2009

CHAPTER 36

When Things Fall Apart

O N MARCH 19, 2009, THE *New York Times* REPORTED: "THE Fed said it would purchase an additional $750 billion worth of government-guaranteed mortgage-backed securities, on top of the $500 billion that it is currently in the process of buying. In addition, the Fed said it would buy up to $300 billion worth of longer-term Treasury securities over the next six months."

The Federal Reserve says that its additional purchase of more than $1 trillion in existing bonds is part of its plan to revive the economy. Another way to view the Fed's announcement is to see it as a preemptive rescue. Is the Fed rescuing banks from their bond portfolios prior to the destruction of bond prices by inflation?

The answer to this question lies in the answer to the question of how the unprecedented sizes of the FY 2009 and FY 2010 federal budget deficits will be financed. Neither the U.S. savings rate nor the trade surpluses of our major foreign lenders are sufficient.

I know of only two ways of financing the looming monster deficits. One, courtesy of Pam Martens, is that the federal deficits could be financed by further flight from equities and other investments.

This is a possibility. If the mortgage-backed security problem is real and not contrived, the next shock should arise from commercial real estate. Stores are closing in shopping centers, and vacancies are rising in office buildings. Without rents, the mortgages can't be paid.

Another scare and another big drop in the stock market will set off a second "flight to quality" and finance the budget deficits.

The other way is to print money. John Williams (shadowstats.com) thinks that the budget deficits will be financed by monetizing debt. Debt monetization happens when the Federal Reserve buys newly issued U.S. Treasury bonds and pays for the purchase by creating demand deposits for the Treasury. The money supply grows by the amount of Fed purchases of new Treasury debt, which is the same as printing money.

Printing money to finance the government's budget normally leads to high inflation and high interest rates.

The initial impact of the announcement of the Fed's plan to purchase existing debt was to drive up bond prices. However, if the reserves poured into the banking system by the bond purchases result in new money growth, and if the Fed purchases the new debt issues to finance the governments' budget deficits, the outlook for bond prices and the dollar becomes poor.

It will be interesting to see how the currency markets view the problem. The *New York Times* reported that "the dollar plunged about 3 per cent against other major currencies" in response to the Fed's announcement.

If the exchange value of the dollar works its way down, it will complicate the financing of the trade deficit and impact the decisions of foreigners who hold large stocks of U.S. dollar debt. The premier of China recently expressed his concern about the safety of his country's large investment in U.S. dollar debt.

If the U.S. government is forced to print money to cover the high costs of its wars and bailouts, things could fall apart very quickly.

MARCH 23, 2009

CHAPTER 37

How the Economy was Lost

T HE AMERICAN ECONOMY HAS GONE AWAY. IT IS NOT COMING BACK until free trade myths are buried six feet under.

America's 20th century economic success was based on two things. Free trade was not one of them. America's economic success was based on protectionism, which was ensured by the Union victory in the Civil War, and on British indebtedness, which destroyed the British pound as world reserve currency. Following World War II, the U.S. dollar took the role as reserve currency, a privilege that allows the U.S. to pay its international bills in its own currency.

World War II and socialism together ensured that the U.S. economy dominated the world at the mid-20th century. The economies of the rest of the world had been destroyed by war or were stifled by socialism.

The ascendant position of the U.S. economy caused the U.S. government to be relaxed about giving away American industries, such as textiles, as bribes to other countries for cooperating with America's cold war and foreign policies. For example, Turkey's U.S. textile quotas were increased in exchange for over-flight rights in the Gulf War, making lost U.S. textile jobs an off-budget war expense.

In contrast, countries such as Japan and Germany used industrial policy to plot their comebacks. By the late 1970s, Japanese auto makers had the once dominant American auto industry on the ropes. The first economic act of the "free market" Reagan administration in 1981 was to put quotas on the import of Japanese cars in order to protect Detroit and the United Auto Workers.

Eamonn Fingleton, Pat Choate, and others have described how negligence in Washington, D.C. aided and abetted the erosion of America's economic position. What we didn't give away, the United States let be taken away while preaching a "free trade" doctrine at which the rest of the world scoffed.

Fortunately, the U.S.'s adversaries at the time, the Soviet Union and China, had unworkable economic systems that posed no threat to America's diminishing economic prowess.

This furlough from reality ended when Soviet, Chinese, and Indian socialism surrendered around 1990, to be followed shortly thereafter by the rise of the high speed Internet. Suddenly, American and other First World corporations discovered that a massive supply of foreign labor was available at practically free wages.

To get Wall Street analysts and shareholder advocacy groups off their backs, and to boost shareholder returns and management bonuses, American corporations began moving their production for American markets offshore. Products that were made in Peoria are now made in China.

As offshoring spread, American cities and states lost tax base, and families and communities lost jobs. The replacement jobs, such as selling the offshored products at Wal-Mart, brought home less pay.

"Free market economists" covered up the damage done to the U.S. economy by preaching a New Economy based on services and innovation. But it wasn't long before corporations discovered that the high speed Internet let them offshore a wide range of professional service jobs. In America, the hardest hit have been software engineers and information technology (IT) workers.

The American corporations quickly learned that by declaring "shortages" of skilled Americans, they could get from Congress H-1B work visas for lower paid foreigners with whom to replace their American work force. Many U.S. corporations are known for forcing their U.S. employees to train their foreign replacements in exchange for severance pay.

Chasing after shareholder return and "performance bonuses," U.S. corporations deserted their American workforce. The consequences can be seen everywhere. The loss of tax base has threatened the municipal bonds of cities and states and reduced the wealth of individuals who purchased the bonds. The lost jobs with good pay resulted in the expansion of consumer debt in order to maintain consumption. As the offshored goods and services are brought back to America to sell, the U.S. trade deficit has exploded to unimaginable heights, calling into question the U.S. dollar as reserve currency and America's ability to finance its trade and budget deficits.

As the American economy eroded away bit by bit, "free market" ideologues produced endless reassurances that America had pulled a fast one on China, sending China dirty and grimy manufacturing jobs. Free of these "old economy" jobs, Americans were lulled with promises of riches. In place of dirty fingernails, American efforts would flow into innovation and entrepreneurship. In the meantime, the "service economy" of software and communications would provide a leg up for the work force.

Education was the answer to all challenges. This appeased the academics, and they produced no studies that would contradict the propaganda and, thus, curtail the flow of federal government and corporate grants.

The "free market" economists, who provided the propaganda and disinformation that hid the act of destroying the U.S. economy, were well paid. As *Business Week* noted, "outsourcing's inner circle has deep roots in General Electric and McKinsey," a consulting firm. Indeed, one of McKinsey's main apologists for offshoring of U.S. jobs, Diane Farrell, is now a member of Obama's White House National Economic Council.

The pressure on U.S. employment from jobs offshoring, together with vast imports, has destroyed the economic prospects for all Americans, except the CEOs who receive "performance" bonuses for moving American jobs offshore or giving them to H-1B work visa holders.

Lowly paid offshored employees, together with H-1B visas, have curtailed employment for new American graduates and for older and more experienced American workers. Older workers traditionally receive higher pay. However, when the determining factor is minimizing labor costs for the sake of shareholder returns and management bonuses, older workers are unaffordable. Doing a good job and providing a good service have ceased to be grounds for employment in corporations that no longer have any loyalty to employees. Instead, the goal is to minimize labor costs at all cost in order to please Wall Street and shareholders. In this way U.S. corporations become the benefactors of foreigners.

"Free trade" has destroyed the employment prospects of older workers. Forced out of their careers, they seek employment as shelf stockers for Wal-Mart where they are paid the minimum wage and no benefits.

I have read endless tributes to Wal-Mart from "libertarian economists," who sing Wal-Mart's praises for bringing low price goods, 70 per cent of which are made in China, to the American consumer. What these "economists" do not factor into their analysis is the diminution of American family incomes and government tax base from the loss of the goods producing jobs to China. Ladders of upward mobility are being dismantled by offshoring, while California issues IOUs to pay its bills. The shift of production offshore reduces GDP. When the goods and services are brought back to America to be sold, they increase the trade deficit. As the trade deficit is financed by foreigners acquiring ownership of U.S. assets, this means that profits, dividends, capital gains, interest, rents, and tolls leave American pockets for foreign ones.

The demise of America's productive economy left the U.S. economy dependent on finance, in which the U.S. remained dominant because the dollar is the reserve currency. With the departure of factories, finance went in new directions. Mortgages, which were once held in the portfolios of the issuer, were securitized and sold.

Individual mortgage debts were combined into a "security." The next step was to strip out the interest payments to the mortgages and sell them as derivatives, thus creating a third debt instrument based on the original mortgages.

In pursuit of ever more profits, financial institutions began betting on the success and failure of various debt instruments and on firms. They bought and sold collateral debt obligations and credit default swaps. A buyer pays a premium to a seller for a swap to guarantee an asset's value. If an asset "insured" by a swap falls in value, the seller of the swap is supposed to make the owner of the swap whole. The purchaser of a swap is not required to own the asset in order to contract for a guarantee of its value. Therefore, as many people could purchase as many swaps as they wished on the same asset. Thus, the total value of the swaps greatly exceeds the value of the assets.

The next step is for holders of the swaps to short the asset in order to drive down its value and collect the guarantee. As the issuers of swaps were not required to reserve against them, and as there is no limit to the number of swaps, the payouts could easily exceed the net worth of the issuer.

This was the most shameful and most mindless form of speculation. Gamblers were betting hands that could not be covered. The U.S. regulators fled their posts. The American financial institutions abandoned all integrity. As a consequence, American financial institutions and rating agencies are trusted nowhere on earth.

The U.S. government should never have used billions of taxpayers' dollars to pay off swap bets as it did when it bailed out the insurance company AIG. This was a stunning waste of a vast sum of money. The federal government should declare all swap agreements to be fraudulent contracts, except for a single swap held by the owner of the asset. Simply wiping out these fraudulent contracts would remove the bulk of the vast overhang of "troubled" assets that threaten financial markets.

The billions of taxpayers' dollars spent buying up subprime derivatives were also wasted. The government did not need to spend one dime. All government needed to do was to suspend the mark-to-market rule. This simple act would have removed the solvency threat to financial institutions by allowing them to keep the derivatives at book value until financial institutions could ascertain their true values and write them down over time.

Taxpayers, equity owners, and the credit standing of the U.S. government are being ruined by financial shysters who are manipulating to their own advantage the government's commitments to mark-to-market and the "sanctity of contracts." Multi trillion dollar "bailouts" and bank nationalization are the result of the U.S. government's inability to respond intelligently.

Two more simple acts would have completed the rescue without costing the taxpayers one dollar: an announcement from the Federal Reserve that it will be lender of last resort to all depository institutions including money market funds, and an announcement reinstating the uptick rule.

The Uptick rule was suspended or repealed a couple of years ago in order to permit hedge funds and shyster speculators to rip-off American equity owners. The rule prevented short-selling any stock that did not move up in price during the previous trade. In other words, speculators could not make money at others' expense by ganging up on a stock and short-selling it trade after trade.

As a former Treasury official, I am amazed that the U.S. government, in the midst of the worst financial crises ever, is content for short-selling to drive down the asset prices that the government is trying to support. No bailout or stimulus plan has any hope until the Uptick rule is reinstated.

The bald fact is that the combination of ignorance, negligence, and ideology that permitted the crisis to happen still prevails and is blocking any remedy. Either the people in power in Washington and the financial community are total dimwits or they are manipulating an opportunity to redistribute wealth from taxpayers, equity owners, and pension funds to financial manipulators.

The Bush and Obama plans total $1.6 trillion, every one of which will have to be borrowed, and no one knows from where. This huge sum will compromise the value of the U.S. dollar, its role as reserve currency, the ability of the U.S. government to service its debt, and the price level. These staggering costs are pointless and are to no avail, as not one step has been taken that would alleviate the crisis.

If we add to my simple menu of remedies a ban against short selling any national currency, the world can be rescued from the current crisis without years of suffering, violent upheavals, and, perhaps, wars.

According to its hopeful but economically ignorant proponents, globalism was supposed to balance risks across national economies and to offset downturns in one part of the world with upturns in other parts. A global portfolio was a protection against loss, claimed globalism's purveyors. In fact, globalism has concentrated the risks, resulting in Wall Street's greed endangering all the economies of the world. The greed of Wall Street and the negligence of the U.S. government have wrecked the prospects of many nations. Street riots are already occurring in parts of the world. On Sunday February 22, the right-wing TV station, Fox

"News," presented a program that predicted riots and disarray in the United States by 2014.

How long will Americans permit "their" government to rip them off for the sake of the financial interests that caused the problem? Obama's cabinet and National Economic Council are filled with representatives of the interest groups that caused the problem. The Obama administration is not a government capable of preventing a worse catastrophe.

If truth be known, the "banking problem" is the least of our worries. Our economy faces two much more serious problems. One is that offshoring and H-1B visas have stopped the growth of family incomes, except, of course, for the super rich. To keep the economy going, consumers have gone deeper into debt, maxing out their credit cards and refinancing their homes and spending the equity. Consumers are now so indebted that they cannot increase their spending by taking on more debt. Thus, whether or not the banks resume lending is beside the point.

The other serious problem is the status of the U.S. dollar as reserve currency. This status has allowed the U.S., now a country heavily dependent on imports just like a Third World or lesser-developed country, to pay its international bills in its own currency. We are able to import $800 billion annually more than we produce, because the foreign countries from whom we import are willing to accept paper for their goods and services.

If the dollar loses its reserve currency role, foreigners will not accept dollars in exchange for real things. This event would be immensely disruptive to an economy dependent on imports for its energy, its clothes, its shoes, its manufactured products, and its advanced technology products.

If incompetence in Washington, the type of incompetence that produced the current economic crisis, destroys the dollar as reserve currency, the "unipower" will overnight become a Third World country, unable to pay for its imports or to sustain its standard of living.

How long can the U.S. government protect the dollar's value by leasing its gold to bullion dealers who sell it, thereby holding down the gold price? Given the incompetence in Washington and on Wall Street, our best hope is that the rest of the world is even less competent and even in deeper trouble. In this event, the U.S. dollar might survive as the least valueless of the world's fiat currencies.

FEBRUARY 24, 2009

CHAPTER 38

The Economy is a Lie, Too

AMERICANS CANNOT GET ANY TRUTH OUT OF THEIR GOVERNMENT about anything, the economy included. Americans are being driven into the ground economically, with one million school children now homeless, while Federal Reserve chairman Ben Bernanke announces that the recession is over.

The spin that masquerades as news is becoming more delusional. Consumer spending is 70 per cent of the U.S. economy. It is the driving force, and it has been shut down. Except for the super rich, there has been no growth in consumer incomes in the 21st century. Statistician John Williams reports that real household income has never recovered its pre-2001 peak.

The U.S. economy has been kept going by substituting growth in consumer debt for growth in consumer income. When he was Federal Reserve chairman Alan Greenspan had encouraged consumer debt with low interest rates. The low interest rates pushed up home prices, enabling Americans to refinance their homes and spend the equity. Credit cards were maxed out in expectations of rising real estate and equity values to pay the accumulated debt. The binge was halted when the real estate and equity bubbles burst.

As consumers no longer can expand their indebtedness and their incomes are not rising, there is no basis for a growing consumer economy. Indeed, statistics indicate that consumers are paying down debt in their efforts to survive financially. In an economy in which the consumer is the driving force, that is bad news.

The banks, now investment banks thanks to greed-driven deregulation that repealed the learned lessons of the past, were even more reckless than consumers and took speculative leverage to new heights. At the urging of Larry Summers and Goldman Sachs' CEO Henry Paulson, the Securities and Exchange Commission and the Bush administration went along with removing restrictions on debt leverage.

When the bubble burst, the extraordinary leverage threatened the financial system with collapse. The U.S. Treasury and the Federal Reserve stepped forward with no one knows how many trillions of dollars to "save the financial system," which, of course, meant to save the greed-driven financial institutions that had caused the economic crisis that dispossessed ordinary Americans of half of their life savings.

The consumer has been chastened, but not the banks. Refreshed with the TARP $700 billion and the Federal Reserve's expanded balance sheet, banks are again behaving like hedge funds. Leveraged speculation is producing another bubble with the current stock market rally, which is not a sign of economic recovery but is the final savaging of Americans' wealth by a few investment banks and their Washington friends. Goldman Sachs, rolling in profits, announced six figure bonuses to employees.

The rest of America is suffering terribly.

The reported unemployment rate does not include jobless Americans who have been unemployed for more than a year and have given up on finding work. As each month passes, unemployed Americans drop off the unemployment role due to nothing except the passing of time.

The inflation rate, especially "core inflation," is another fiction. "Core inflation" does not include food and energy, two of Americans' biggest budget items. The Consumer Price Index (CPI) assumes, ever since the Boskin Commission during the Clinton administration, that if prices of items go up consumers substitute cheaper items. This is certainly the case, but this way of measuring inflation means that the CPI is no longer comparable to past years, because the basket of goods in the index is variable.

The Boskin Commission's CPI, by lowering the measured rate of inflation, raises the real GDP growth rate. The result of the statistical manipulation is an understated inflation rate, thus eroding the real value of Social Security income, and an overstated growth rate. Statistical manipulation cloaks a declining standard of living.

In bygone days of American prosperity, American incomes rose with productivity. It was the real growth in American incomes that propelled the U.S. economy.

In today's America, the only incomes that rise are in the financial sector that risks the country's future on excessive leverage and in the corporate world that substitutes foreign for American labor. Under the compensation rules and emphasis on shareholder earnings that hold sway in the U.S. today, corporate executives maximize earnings and their compensation by minimizing the employment of Americans.

Try to find some acknowledgement of this in the "mainstream media," or among economists, who suck up to the offshoring corporations for grants.

The worst part of the decline is yet to come. Bank failures and home foreclosures are yet to peak. The commercial real estate bust is yet to hit. The dollar crisis is building. When it hits, interest rates will rise dramatically as the U.S. struggles to finance its massive budget and trade deficits while the rest of the world tries to escape a depreciating dollar.

Since the spring of 2009, the value of the U.S. dollar has collapsed against every currency except those pegged to it. The Swiss franc has risen 14 per cent against the dollar. Every hard currency from the Canadian dollar to the Euro and U.K. pound has risen at least 13 per cent against the U.S. dollar since April 2009. The Japanese yen is not far behind, and the Brazilian real has risen 25 per cent against the almighty U.S. dollar. Even the Russian ruble has risen 13 per cent against the U.S. dollar.

What sort of recovery is it when the safest investment is to bet against the U.S. dollar?

The American household of my day, in which the husband worked and the wife provided household services and raised the children, scarcely exists today. Most, if not all, members of a household have to work in order to pay the bills. However, the jobs are disappearing, even the part-time ones.

If measured according to the methodology used when I was Assistant Secretary of the Treasury, the unemployment rate today in the U.S. is 21.4 per cent. Moreover, there is no obvious way of reducing it. There are no factories, with work forces temporarily laid off by high interest rates, waiting for a lower interest rate policy to call their workforces back into production.

The work has been moved abroad. In the bygone days of American prosperity, CEOs were inculcated with the view that they had equal responsibilities to customers, employees, and shareholders. This view has been exterminated. Pushed by Wall Street and the threat of takeovers promising "enhanced shareholder value," and incentivized by "performance pay," CEOs use every means to substitute cheaper foreign employees for Americans. Despite 20 per cent unemployment and *cum laude* engineering graduates who cannot find jobs or even job interviews, Congress continues to support 65,000 annual H-1B work visas for foreigners.

In the midst of the highest unemployment since the Great Depression what kind of a fool do you need to be to think that there is a shortage of qualified U.S. workers?

SEPTEMBER 23, 2009

CHAPTER 39

As the Dollar Sinks
—A Perfect Storm

ECONOMIC NEWS REMAINS FOCUSED ON BANKS AND HOUSING, WHILE the threat mounts to the U.S. dollar from massive federal budget deficits in fiscal years 2009 and 2010.

Earlier this year the dollar's exchange value rose against currencies, such as the euro, U.K. pound, and Swiss franc, against which the dollar had been steadily falling. The dollar's rise made U.S. policymakers complacent, even though the rise was due to flight from over-leveraged financial instruments and falling stock markets into "safe" Treasuries. Since April, however, the dollar has steadily declined as investors and foreign central banks realize that the massive federal budget deficits are likely to be monetized.

What happens to the dollar will be the key driver of what lies ahead. The likely scenario could be nasty.

America's trading partners do not have large enough trade surpluses to finance a federal budget deficit swollen to $2 trillion by gratuitous wars, recession, bailouts, and stimulus programs. Moreover, concern over the dollar's future is causing America's foreign creditors to seek alternatives to U.S. debt in which to hold their foreign reserves.

According to a recent report in the online edition of *Pravda*, Russia's central bank now holds a larger proportion of its reserves in euros than in U.S. dollars. On May 18 the *Financial Times* reported that China and Brazil are considering bypassing the dollar and conducting their mutual trade in their own currencies. Other reports say that China has increased its gold reserves by 75 per cent in recent years.

China's premier, Wen Jiabao, has publicly expressed his concern about the future of the dollar. Arrogant, hubris-filled American officials and their yes-men economists discount Chinese warnings, arguing that the Chinese have no choice but to support the dollar by purchasing

Washington's red ink. Otherwise, they say, China stands to lose the value of its large dollar portfolio.

China sees it differently. It is obvious to Chinese officials that neither China nor the entire world has enough spare money to purchase $3 trillion or more of U.S. Treasuries over the next two years. According to the *London Telegraph* on May 27, Dallas Federal Reserve Bank president Richard Fisher was repeatedly grilled by senior officials of the Chinese government during his recent visit about whether the Federal Reserve was going to finance the U.S. budget deficit by printing money. According to Fisher, "I must have been asked about that a hundred times in China. I was asked at every single meeting about our purchases of Treasuries. That seemed to be the principal preoccupation of those that were invested with their surpluses mostly in the United States."

U.S. Treasury Secretary Timothy Geithner has gone to China to calm the fears. However, even before he arrived, a Chinese central bank spokesman gave Geithner the message that the U.S. should not assume China will continue to finance Washington's extravagant budgets. The governor of China's central bank is calling for the abandonment of the dollar as reserve currency, suggesting the use of the International Monetary Fund's Special Drawing Rights in its place.

President Lyndon Johnson's "guns and butter" policy during the 1960s forced president Richard Nixon to eliminate the gold backing that the dollar had as world reserve currency, putting foreign central banks on the same fiat money standard as the U.S. economy. In its first four months, the Obama administration has outdone president Johnson. Instead of ending war, Obama has expanded America's war of aggression in Afghanistan and spread it into Pakistan. War, bailouts, and stimulus plans have pushed the government's annual operating budget 50 per cent into the red.

Washington's financial irresponsibility has brought pressure on the dollar and the U.S. bond market. Federal Reserve Chairman Bernanke thought he could push down interest rates on Treasuries by purchasing $300 billion of them. However, the result was a drop (after a short-lived initial rise) in Treasury prices and a rise in interest rates.

As monetization of federal debt goes forward, U.S. interest rates will continue to rise, worsening the problems in the real estate sector. The dollar will continue to lose value, making it harder for the U.S. to finance its budget and trade deficits. Domestic inflation will raise its ugly head despite high unemployment.

The incompetents who manage U.S. economic policy have created a perfect storm.

The Obama-Federal Reserve-Wall Street plan for the U.S. to spend its way out of its problems is coming unglued. The reckless spending is pushing the dollar down and interest rates up.

Every sector of the U.S. economy is in trouble. Former U.S. manufacturing firms have been turned into marketing companies trying to sell their foreign-made goods to domestic consumers who have seen their jobs moved offshore. Much of what is left of U.S. manufacturing—the auto industry—is in bankruptcy. More decline awaits housing and commercial real estate. The dollar is sliding, and interest rates are rising, despite the Federal Reserve's attempts to hold interest rates down.

When the Reagan administration cured stagflation, the result was a secular bull-market in U.S. Treasuries that lasted 28 years. That bull market is over. Americans' living standards are headed down. The American standard of living has been destroyed by wars, by offshoring of jobs, by financial deregulation, by trillion dollar handouts to financial gangsters who have, so far, destroyed half of Americans' retirement savings, and by the monetization of debt.

The next shoe to drop will be the dollar's loss of the reserve currency role. Then the U.S., an import-dependent country, will no longer be able to pay for its imports. Shortages will worsen price inflation and disrupt deliveries.

Life for most Americans will become truly stressful.

JUNE 3, 2009

CHAPTER 40

What Economy?

HERE IS NO ECONOMY LEFT TO RECOVER. THE U.S. MANUFACTURING economy was lost to offshoring and free trade ideology. It was replaced by a mythical "New Economy."

The "New Economy" was based on services. Its artificial life was fed by the Federal Reserve's artificially low interest rates, which produced a real estate bubble, and by "free market" financial deregulation, which unleashed financial gangsters to new heights of debt leverage and fraudulent financial products.

The real economy was traded away for a make-believe economy. When the make-believe economy collapsed, Americans' wealth in their real estate, pensions, and savings collapsed dramatically while their jobs disappeared.

The debt economy caused Americans to leverage their assets. They refinanced their homes and spent the equity. They maxed out numerous credit cards. They worked as many jobs as they could find. Debt expansion and multiple family incomes kept the economy going.

And now suddenly Americans can't borrow in order to spend. They are over their heads in debt. Jobs are disappearing. America's consumer economy, approximately 70 per cent of GDP, is dead. Those Americans who still have jobs are saving against the prospect of job loss. Millions are homeless. Some have moved in with family and friends; others are living in tent cities and in their cars.

Meanwhile the U.S. government's budget deficit has jumped from $455 billion in 2008 to $1.42 trillion this year, with another $1,500 billion on the books for 2010. And President Obama has intensified America's expensive war of aggression in Afghanistan and initiated a new war in Pakistan.

There is no way for these deficits to be financed except by printing money or by further collapse in stock markets that would drive people out of equity into bonds.

The U.S. government's budget is 50 per cent in the red. That means half of every dollar the federal government spends must be borrowed or printed. Because of the worldwide debacle caused by Wall Street's financial gangsterism, the world needs its own money and hasn't $1.5 trillion annually to lend to Washington.

As dollars are printed, the growing supply adds to the pressure on the dollar's role as reserve currency. Already America's largest creditor, China, is admonishing Washington to protect China's investment in U.S. debt and lobbying for a new reserve currency to replace the dollar before it collapses. According to various reports, China is spending down its holdings of U.S. dollars by acquiring gold and stocks of raw materials and energy.

The price of one ounce of gold coins is $1,000 despite efforts of the U.S. government to hold down the gold price. How high will this price jump when the rest of the world decides that the bankruptcy of "the world's only superpower" is at hand?

And what will happen to America's ability to import not only oil, but also the manufactured goods on which it is import-dependent?

When the over-supplied U.S. dollar loses the reserve currency role, the U.S. will no longer be able to pay for its massive imports of real goods and services with pieces of paper. Overnight, shortages will appear and Americans will be poorer.

Nothing in Presidents Bush and Obama's economic policy addresses the real issues. Instead, Goldman Sachs was bailed out, more than once. As Eliot Spitzer said, the banks made a "bloody fortune" with U.S. aid.

It was not the millions of now homeless homeowners who were bailed out. It was not the scant remains of American manufacturers that were bailed out. It was the Wall Street banks.

According to Bloomberg.com, Goldman Sachs' current record earnings from their free or low cost capital supplied by broke American taxpayers has led the firm to decide to boost compensation and benefits by 33 per cent. On an annual basis, this comes to compensation of $773,000 per employee.

This should tell even the most dimwitted patriot who "their" government represents.

The worst of the economic crisis has not yet hit. I don't mean the rest of the real estate crisis that is waiting in the wings. Home prices will fall further when the foreclosed properties currently held off the market are dumped. Store and office closings are adversely impacting the ability of owners of shopping malls and office buildings to make their mortgage payments. Commercial real estate loans were also securitized and turned into derivatives.

The real crisis awaits us. It is the crisis of high unemployment, of stagnant and declining real wages confronted with rising prices from the printing of money to pay the government's bills and from the dollar's loss of exchange value.

Retirees dependent on state pension systems, which cannot print money, might not be paid, or might be paid with IOUs. They will not even have depreciating money with which to try to pay their bills. Desperate tax authorities will squeeze the remaining life out of the middle class.

Nothing in Obama's economic policy is directed at saving the U.S. dollar as reserve currency or the livelihoods of the American people. Obama's policy, like Bush's before him, is keyed to the enrichment of Goldman Sachs and the armament industries.

Matt Taibbi describes Goldman Sachs as "a great vampire squid wrapped around the face of humanity, relentlessly jamming its blood funnel into anything that smells like money." Look at the Goldman Sachs representatives in the Clinton, Bush, and Obama administrations. This bankster firm controls the economic policy of the United States.

Little wonder that Goldman Sachs has record earnings while the rest of us grow poorer by the day.

JULY 16, 2009

CHAPTER 41

The Expiring Economy

TENT CITIES SPRINGING UP ALL OVER AMERICA ARE FILLING WITH the homeless unemployed from the worst economy since the 1930s. While Americans live in tents, the Obama government has embarked on a $1 billion crash program to build a mega-embassy in Islamabad, Pakistan, to rival the one the Bush government built in Baghdad, Iraq.

Hard times have now afflicted Americans for so long that even the extension of unemployment benefits from 6 months to 18 months for 24 high unemployment states, and to 46–72 weeks in other states, is beginning to run out. By Christmas 2009, 1.5 million Americans will have exhausted unemployment benefits while unemployment rolls continue to rise.

Amidst this worsening economic crisis, the House of Representatives just passed a $636 billion "defense" bill.

Who is the United States defending against? Americans have no enemies except those that the U.S. government goes out of its way to create by bombing and invading countries that comprise no threat whatsoever to the U.S. and by encircling others—Russia for example—with threatening military bases.

America's wars are contrived affairs to serve the money laundering machine: from the taxpayers and money borrowed from foreign creditors to the armaments industry to the political contributions that ensure $636 billion "defense" bills.

President George W. Bush gave us wars in Iraq and Afghanistan that are entirely based on lies and misrepresentations. But Obama has done Bush one better. Obama has started a war in Pakistan with no explanation whatsoever.

If the armaments industry and the neoconservative brownshirts have their way, the U.S. will also be at war with Iran, Russia, Sudan, and North Korea.

Meanwhile, America continues to be overrun, as it has been for decades, not by armed foreign enemies but by illegal immigrants across America's porous and undefended borders.

It is more proof of the Orwellian time in which we live that $636 billion appropriated for wars of aggression is called a "defense bill."

Who is going to pay for all of this? When foreign countries have spent their trade surpluses and have no more dollars to recycle into the purchase of Treasury bonds, when U.S. banks have used up their "bailout" money by purchasing Treasury bonds, and when the Federal Reserve cannot print any more money to keep the government going without pushing up inflation and interest rates, the taxpayer will be all that is left. Already Obama's two top economic advisors, Treasury Secretary Timothy Geithner and director of the National Economic Council Larry Summers, are floating the prospect of a middle class tax increase. Will Obama be maneuvered away from his promise just as Bush Sr. was?

Will Americans see the disconnect between their interests and the interests of "their" government? In the small town of Vassalboro, Maine, a few topless waitress jobs in a coffee house drew 150 applicants. Women in this small town are so desperate for jobs that they are reduced to undressing for their neighbors' amusement.

Meanwhile, the Obama government is going to straighten out Afghanistan and Pakistan and build marble palaces to awe the locals half way around the world.

The U.S. government keeps hyping "recovery" the way Bush hyped "terrorist threat" and "weapons of mass destruction." The recovery is no more real than the threats. Indeed, it is possible that the economic collapse has hardly begun. Let's look at what might await us here at home while the U.S. government pursues hegemony abroad.

The real estate crisis is not over. More home foreclosures await as unemployment rises and unemployment benefits are exhausted. The commercial real estate crisis is yet to hit. More bailouts are coming, and they will have to be financed by more debt or money creation. If there are not sufficient purchasers for the Treasury bonds, the Federal Reserve will have to purchase them by creating checking accounts for the Treasury, that is, by debt monetization or the printing of money.

More debt and money creation will put more pressure on the U.S. dollar's exchange value. At some point import prices, which include off-shored goods and services of U.S. corporations, will rise, adding to the inflation fueled by domestic money creation. The Federal Reserve will be unable to hold down interest rates by buying bonds.

No part of U.S. economic policy addresses the systemic crisis in American incomes. For most Americans real income ceased to grow some years ago. Americans have substituted second jobs and debt accumulation for the missing growth in real wages. With most households maxed out on debt and jobs disappearing, these substitutes for real income growth no longer exist.

The Bush-Obama economic policy actually worsens the systemic crisis that the U.S. dollar faces as reserve currency. The fact that there might be no alternative to the dollar as reserve currency does not guarantee that the dollar will continue in this role. Countries might find it less risky to settle trade transactions in their own currencies.

How does an economy based heavily on consumer spending recover when so many high-value-added jobs, and the GDP and payroll tax revenues associated with them, have been moved offshore and when consumers have no more assets to leverage in order to increase their spending?

How does the U.S. pay for its imports if the dollar is no longer used as reserve currency?

These are the unanswered questions.

AUGUST 6, 2009

CHAPTER 42

Marx and Lenin Reconsidered

> "Capital is dead labor, which, vampire-like, lives only by sucking living labor, and lives the more, the more labor it sucks."—Karl Marx

I F KARL MARX AND V. I. LENIN WERE ALIVE TODAY, THEY WOULD BE leading contenders for the Nobel Prize in economics.

Marx predicted the growing misery of working people, and Lenin foresaw the subordination of the production of goods to financial capital's accumulation of profits based on the purchase and sale of paper instruments. Their predictions are far superior to the "risk models" for which the Nobel Prize has been given and are closer to the money than the predictions of Federal Reserve chairmen, U.S. Treasury secretaries, and Nobel economists, such as Paul Krugman, who believe that more credit and more debt are the solution to the economic crisis.

In this first decade of the 21st century there has been no increase in the real incomes of working Americans. There has been a sharp decline in their wealth. In the 21st century Americans have suffered two major stock market crashes and the destruction of their real estate wealth.

Some studies have concluded that the real incomes of Americans, except for the financial oligarchy of the super rich, are less today than in the 1980s and even the 1970s. I have not examined these studies of family income to determine whether they are biased by the rise in divorce and percentage of single parent households. However, for the last decade it is clear that real take-home pay has declined.

The main cause of this decline is the offshoring of U.S. high value-added jobs. Both manufacturing jobs and professional services, such as software engineering and information technology work, have been relocated in countries with large and cheap labor forces.

The wipeout of middle class jobs was disguised by the growth in consumer debt. As Americans' incomes ceased to grow, consumer debt expanded to take the place of income growth and to keep consumer demand rising. Unlike rises in consumer incomes due to productivity growth, there is a limit to debt expansion. When that limit is reached, the economy ceases to grow.

The immiseration of working people has not resulted from worsening crises of over-production of goods and services, but from financial capital's power to force the relocation of production for domestic markets to foreign shores. Wall Street's pressures, including pressures from takeovers, forced American manufacturing firms to "increase shareholders' earnings." This was done by substituting cheap foreign labor for American labor.

Corporations offshored or outsourced abroad their manufacturing output, thus divorcing American incomes from the production of the goods that they consume. The next step in the process took advantage of the high speed Internet to move professional service jobs, such as engineering, abroad. The third step was to replace the remains of the domestic work force with foreigners on H-1B, L-1, and other work visas.

This process by which financial capital destroyed the job prospects of Americans was covered up by "free market" economists, who received grants from offshoring firms in exchange for propaganda that Americans would benefit from a "New Economy" based on financial services, and by shills in the education business, who justified work visas for foreigners on the basis of the lie that America produces a shortage of engineers and scientists.

In Marx's day, religion was the opiate of the masses. Today the media is. Let's look at media reporting that facilitates the financial oligarchy's ability to delude the people.

The financial oligarchy is hyping a recovery while American unemployment and home foreclosures are rising. The hype owes its credibility to the high positions from which it comes, to the problems in payroll jobs reporting that overstate employment, and to disposal into the memory hole of any American unemployed for more than one year.

On October 2, 2009, statistician John Williams of shadowstats.com reported that the Bureau of Labor Statistics has announced a preliminary estimate of its annual benchmark revision of 2009 employment.

The BLS has found that employment in 2009 has been overstated by about one million jobs. John Williams believes the overstatement is two million jobs. He reports that "the birth-death model currently adds [an illusory] net gain of about 900,000 jobs per year to payroll employment reporting."

The non-farm payroll number is always the headline report. However, Williams believes that the household survey of unemployment is statistically sounder than the payroll survey. The BLS has never been able to reconcile the difference in the numbers in the two employment surveys. On October 2, the headline payroll number of lost jobs was 263,000 for the month of September. However the household survey number was 785,000 lost jobs in the month of September.

The headline unemployment rate of 9.8 per cent is a bare bones measure that greatly understates unemployment. Government reporting agencies know this and report another unemployment number, known as U-6. This measure of U.S. unemployment stands at 17 per cent in September 2009.

When the long-term discouraged workers are added back into the total unemployed, the unemployment rate in September 2009 stands at 21.4 per cent.

The unemployment of American citizens could actually be even higher. When Microsoft or some other firm replaces several thousand U.S. workers with foreigners on H-1B visas, Microsoft does not report a decline in payroll employment. Nevertheless, several thousand Americans are now without jobs. Multiply this by the number of U.S. firms that are relying on "body shops" to replace their U.S. work force with cheap foreign labor year after year, and the result is hundreds of thousands of unreported unemployed Americans.

Obviously, with more than one-fifth of the American work force unemployed and the remainder buried in mortgage and credit card debt, economic recovery is not in the picture.

What is happening is that the hundreds of billions of dollars in TARP money given to the large banks and the trillions of dollars that have been added to the Federal Reserve's balance sheet have been funneled into the stock market, producing another bubble, and into the acquisition of smaller banks by banks "too large to fail." The result is more financial concentration.

The expansion in debt that underlies this bubble has further eroded the U.S. dollar's credibility as reserve currency. When the dollar starts to go, panicked policy-makers will raise interest rates in order to protect the U.S. Treasury's borrowing capability. When the interest rates rise, what little remains of the U.S. economy will tank.

If the government cannot borrow, it will print money to pay its bills. Hyperinflation will hit the American population. Massive unemployment and massive inflation will inflict upon the American people misery that not even Marx and Lenin could envisage.

Meanwhile America's economists continue to pretend that they are dealing with a normal postwar recession that merely requires an expansion of money and credit to restore economic growth.

OCTOBER 7, 2009

CHAPTER 43

The Rich Have Stolen the Economy

BLOOMBERG REPORTS THAT TREASURY SECRETARY TIMOTHY Geithner's closest aides earned millions of dollars a year working for Goldman Sachs, Citigroup, and other Wall Street firms. Bloomberg adds that none of these aides faced Senate confirmation. Yet, they are overseeing the handout of hundreds of billions of dollars of taxpayer funds to their former employers.

The gifts of billions of dollars of taxpayers' money provided the banks with an abundance of low cost capital that has boosted the banks' profits, while the taxpayers who provided the capital are increasingly unemployed and homeless.

JP Morgan-Chase announced that it has earned $3.6 billion in the third quarter of 2009.

Goldman Sachs has made so much money during this year of economic crisis that enormous bonuses are in the works. The London *Evening Standard* reports that Goldman Sachs' "5,500 London staff can look forward to record average payouts of around 500,000 pounds ($800,000) each. Senior executives will get bonuses of several million pounds each with the highest paid as much as 10 million pounds ($16 million)."

In the event the banksters can't figure out how to enjoy the riches, the *Financial Times* is offering a magazine—"How To Spend It." New York City's retailers are praying for some of it, suffering a 15.3 per cent vacancy rate on Fifth Avenue. Statistician John Williams reports that retail sales adjusted for inflation have declined to the level of 10 years ago: "Virtually 10 years worth of real retail sales growth has been destroyed in the still unfolding depression."

Meanwhile, occupants of New York City's homeless shelters have reached the all time high of 39,000—16,000 of whom are children.

New York City government is so overwhelmed that it is paying $90 per night per apartment to rent unsold new apartments for the homeless.

Desperate, the city government is offering one-way free airline tickets to the homeless if they will leave the city. It is charging rent to shelter residents who have jobs. A single mother earning $800 per month is paying $336 in shelter rent.

Long-term unemployment has become a serious problem across the country, more than doubling the unemployment rate from the reported 10 per cent to 21.4 per cent. Now hundreds of thousands more Americans are beginning to run out of extended unemployment benefits. High unemployment has made 2009 a banner year for military recruitment.

A record number of Americans, more than one in nine, are on food stamps. Mortgage delinquencies are rising as home prices fall. According to Jay Brinkmann of the Mortgage Bankers Association, job losses have spread the problem from subprime loans to prime fixed-rate loans. At the Wise, Virginia fairgrounds, 2,000 people waited in lines for free dental and health care.

While the U.S. speeds plans for the ultimate bunker buster bomb and President Obama prepares to send another 45,000 troops into Afghanistan, 44,789 Americans die every year from lack of medical treatment. National Guardsmen say they would rather face the Taliban than the U.S. economy.

Little wonder. In the midst of the worst unemployment since the Great Depression, U.S. corporations continue to offshore jobs and to replace their remaining U.S. employees with lower paid foreigners on work visas.

The offshoring of jobs, the bailout of rich banksters, and war deficits are destroying the value of the U.S. dollar. Since last spring the U.S. dollar has been rapidly losing value. The currency of the hegemonic superpower has declined 14 per cent against the Botswana pula, 22 per cent against Brazil's real, and 11 per cent against the Russian ruble. Once the dollar loses its reserve currency status, the U.S. will be unable to pay for its imports or to finance its government budget deficits.

Offshoring has made Americans heavily dependent on imports, and the dollar's loss of purchasing power will further erode American incomes. As the Federal Reserve is forced to monetize Treasury debt issues, domestic inflation will break out. Except for the banksters and the offshoring CEOs, there is no source of consumer demand to drive the U.S. economy.

The political system is unresponsive to the American people. It is monopolized by a few powerful interest groups that control campaign contributions. Interest groups have exercised their power to monopolize the economy for the benefit of themselves, the American people be damned.

OCTOBER 16, 2009

CHAPTER 44

Are You Ready for the Next Crisis?

EVIDENCE THAT THE U.S. IS A FAILED STATE IS PILING UP FASTER than I can record it.

One conclusive hallmark of a failed state is that the crooks are inside the government, using government to protect and to advance their private interests.

Another conclusive hallmark is rising income inequality as the insiders manipulate economic policy for their enrichment at the expense of everyone else.

Income inequality in the U.S. is now the most extreme of all countries. The 2008 OECD report, "Income Distribution and Poverty in OECD Countries," concludes that the U.S. is the country with the highest inequality and poverty rate across the OECD and that since 2000 nowhere has there been such a stark rise in income inequality as in the U.S. The OECD finds that in the U.S. the distribution of wealth is even more unequal than the distribution of income.

On October 21, 2009, *Business Week* highlighted a new report from the United Nations Development Program. The report concluded that the U.S. ranked third among states with the worst income inequality. As number one and number two, Hong Kong and Singapore are both essentially city states, not countries. The U.S. actually has the shame of being the country with the most inequality in the distribution of income.

The stark increase in U.S. income inequality in the 21st century coincides with the offshoring of U.S. jobs, which enriched executives with "performance bonuses" while impoverishing the middle class, and with the rapid rise of unregulated OTC derivatives, which enriched Wall Street and the financial sector at the expense of everyone else.

Millions of Americans have lost their homes and half of their retirement savings while being loaded up with government debt to bail out the banksters who created the derivative crisis.

Frontline's October 21, 2009, broadcast, "The Warning," documents how Federal Reserve Chairman Alan Greenspan, Treasury Secretary Robert Rubin, Deputy Treasury Secretary Larry Summers, and Securities and Exchange Commission Chairman Arthur Levitt blocked Brooksley Born, head of the Commodity Futures Trading Commission, from performing her statutory duties and regulating OTC derivatives.

After the worst crisis in U.S. financial history struck, just as Brooksley Born said it would, a disgraced Alan Greenspan was summoned out of retirement to explain to Congress his unequivocal assurances that no regulation of derivatives was necessary. Greenspan had even told Congress that regulation of derivatives would be harmful. A pathetic Greenspan had to admit that the free market ideology on which he had relied turned out to have a flaw.

Greenspan may have bet our country on his free market ideology, but does anyone believe that Rubin and Summers were doing anything other than protecting the enormous fraud-based profits that derivatives were bringing Wall Street? As Brooksley Born stressed, OTC derivatives are a "dark market." There is no transparency. Regulators have no information on them and neither do purchasers.

Even after Long Term Capital Management blew up in 1998 and had to be bailed out, Greenspan, Rubin, and Summers stuck to their guns. Greenspan, Rubin and Summers, and a roped-in gullible Arthur Levitt who now regrets that he was the banksters' dupe, succeeded in manipulating a totally ignorant Congress into blocking the CFTC from doing its mandated job. Brooksley Born, prevented by the public's elected representatives from protecting the public, resigned. Wall Street money simply shoved facts and honest regulators aside, guaranteeing government inaction and the financial crisis that hit in 2008 and continues to plague our economy today.

The financial insiders running the Treasury, White House, and Federal Reserve shifted to taxpayers the cost of the catastrophe that they had created. When the crisis hit, Henry Paulson, appointed by President Bush as Rubin's replacement as the Goldman Sachs representative running the U.S. Treasury, hyped fear to obtain from "our" representatives in Congress, with no questions, asked hundreds of billions of taxpayers' dollars (TARP money) to bail out Goldman Sachs and the other malefactors of unregulated derivatives.

When Goldman Sachs recently announced that it was paying massive six and seven figure bonuses to every employee, public outrage erupted. In defense of banksters, saved with the public's money, paying themselves bonuses in excess of most people's life-time earnings, Lord Griffiths, Vice Chairman of Goldman Sachs International, said that the public must learn to "tolerate the inequality as a way to achieve greater prosperity for all."

In other words, "Let them eat cake."

According to the UN report cited above, Great Britain has the seventh most unequal income distribution in the world. After the Goldman Sachs bonuses, the British will move up in distinction, perhaps rivaling Israel for the fourth spot in the hierarchy.

Despite the total insanity of unregulated derivatives, the high level of public anger, and Greenspan's confession to Congress, still nothing has been done to regulate derivatives. One of Rubin's Assistant Treasury Secretaries, Gary Gensler, has replaced Brooksley Born as head of the CFTC. Larry Summers is the head of President Obama's National Economic Council. Former Federal Reserve official Timothy Geithner, a Paulson protege, runs the Obama Treasury. A Goldman Sachs vice president, Adam Storch, has been appointed the chief operating officer of the Securities and Exchange Commission. The Banksters are still in charge.

Is there another country in which, in full public view, so few so blatantly use government for the enrichment of private interests, with a coterie of "free market" economists available to justify plunder on the grounds that "the market knows best"? A narco-state is bad enough. The U.S. surpasses this horror with its financo-state.

As Brooksley Born says, if nothing is done "it'll happen again."

But nothing can be done. The crooks have the government.

Note: The OECD report shows that despite the Reagan tax rate reduction, the rate of increase in U.S. income inequality declined during the Reagan years. During the mid-1990s the Gini coefficient (the measure of income inequality) actually fell. Beginning in 2000 with the New

Economy (essentially financial fraud and offshoring of U.S. jobs), the Gini coefficient shot up sharply.

OCTOBER 26, 2009

CHAPTER 45

My "Epiphany"

A NUMBER OF READERS HAVE ASKED ME WHEN DID I UNDERGO my epiphany, abandon right-wing Reaganism and become an apostle of truth and justice.

I appreciate the friendly sentiment, but there is a great deal of misconception in the question.

When I saw that the neoconservative response to 9/11 was to turn a war against stateless terrorism into military attacks on Muslim states, I realized that the Bush administration was committing a strategic blunder with open-ended disastrous consequences for the U.S. that, in the end, would destroy Bush, the Republican Party, and the conservative movement.

My warning was not prompted by an effort to save Bush's bacon. I have never been any party's political or ideological servant. I used my positions in the congressional staff and the Reagan administration to change the economic policy of the United States. In my efforts, I found more allies among influential Democrats, such as Senate Finance Committee Chairman Russell Long, Joint Economic Committee Chairman Lloyd Bentsen, and my Georgia Tech fraternity brother Sam Nunn, than I did among traditional Republicans who were only concerned about the budget deficit.

My goals were to reverse the Keynesian policy mix that caused worsening "Phillips curve" trade-offs between employment and inflation and to cure the stagflation that destroyed Jimmy Carter's presidency. No one has seen a "Phillips curve" trade-off or experienced stagflation since the supply-side policy was implemented.

The supply-side policy used reductions in the marginal rate of taxation on additional income to create incentives to expand production so that consumer demand would result in increased real output instead of higher prices. No doubt, the rich benefited, but ordinary people were no longer faced simultaneously with rising inflation and lost jobs.

Employment expanded for the remainder of the century without having to pay for it with high and rising rates of inflation. Don't ever forget that Reagan was elected and re-elected by blue collar Democrats.

The left-wing's demonization of Ronald Reagan owes much to the Republican Establishment. The Republican Establishment regarded Reagan as a threat to its hegemony over the party. They saw Jack Kemp the same way. Kemp, a professional football star quarterback, represented an essentially Democratic district. Kemp was aggressive in challenging Republican orthodoxy. Both Reagan and Kemp spoke to ordinary people. As a high official in the Reagan administration, I was battered by the Republican Establishment, which wanted enough Reagan success so as not to jeopardize the party's "lock on the presidency" but enough failure so as to block the succession to another outsider. Anyone who reads my book, *The Supply-Side Revolution* (Harvard University Press, 1984), will see what the real issues were.

If I had time to research my writings over the past 30 years, I could find examples of partisan articles on behalf of Republicans and against Democrats. However, political partisanship is not the corpus of my writings. I had a 16-year-stint as *Business Week*'s first outside columnist, despite hostility within the magazine and from the editor's New York social set, because the editor regarded me as the most trenchant critic of the George H.W. Bush administration in the business. The White House felt the same way and lobbied to have me removed from the William E. Simon Chair in Political Economy at the Center for Strategic and International Studies.

Earlier when I resigned from the Reagan administration to accept appointment to the new chair, CSIS was part of Georgetown University. The university's liberal president, Timothy Healy, objected to having anyone from the Reagan administration in a chair affiliated with Georgetown University. CSIS had to defuse the situation by appointing a distinguished panel of scholars from outside universities, including Harvard, to ratify my appointment.

I can truly say that at one time or the other both sides have tried to shut me down. I have experienced the same from "free thinking" libertarians, who are free thinking only inside their own box.

In Reagan's time we did not recognize that neoconservatives had a Jacobin frame of mind. Perhaps we were not paying close enough attention. We saw neoconservatives as former left-wingers who had realized that the Soviet Union might be a threat after all. We regarded them as allies against Henry Kissinger's inclination to reach an unfavorable accommodation with the Soviet Union. Kissinger thought, or was believed to think, that Americans had no stomach for a drawn-out contest and that he needed to strike a deal before the Soviets staked the future on a lack of American resolution.

Reagan was certainly no neoconservative. He went along with some of their schemes, but when neoconservatives went too far, he fired them. George W. Bush promotes them. The left-wing might object that the offending neocons in the Reagan administration were later pardoned, but there was sincere objection to criminalizing what was seen, rightly or wrongly, as stalwartness in standing up to communism.

Neoconservatives were disappointed with Reagan. Reagan's goal was to *end* the cold war, not to *win* it. He made common purpose with Gorbachev and *ended* the cold war. It is the new Jacobins, the neoconservatives, who have exploited this victory by taking military bases to Russian borders.

I have always objected to injustice. My writings about prosecutorial abuse have put me at odds with "law and order conservatives." I have written extensively about wrongful convictions, both of the rich and famous and the poor and unknown. My 30-odd columns on the frame-up of 26 innocent people in the Wenatchee, Washington child sex abuse witch hunt played a role in the eventual overturning of the wrongful convictions.

My book, with Lawrence Stratton, *The Tyranny of Good Intentions*, details the erosion of the legal rights that make law a shield of the innocent instead of a weapon in the hands of government. Without the protection of law, rich and poor alike are at the mercy of government.

Americans have forgotten what it takes to remain free. Instead, every ideology, every group is determined to use government to advance its agenda. As the government's power grows, the people are eclipsed.

We have reached a point where the Bush administration is determined to totally eclipse the people. Bewitched by neoconservatives and lustful for power, the Bush administration and the Republican Party are aligning themselves firmly against the American people. Their first victims, of course, were the true conservatives. Having eliminated internal opposition, the Bush administration is now using blackmail obtained through illegal spying on American citizens to silence the media and the opposition party.

Before flinching at my assertion of blackmail, ask yourself why President Bush refuses to obey the Foreign Intelligence Surveillance Act. The purpose of the FISA court is to ensure that administrations do not spy for partisan political reasons. The warrant requirement is to ensure that a panel of independent federal judges hears a legitimate reason for the spying, thus protecting a president from the temptation to abuse the powers of government. The only reason for the Bush administration to evade the court is that the Bush administration had no legitimate reasons for its spying. This should be obvious even to a naif.

The United States is undergoing a coup against the Constitution, the Bill of Rights, civil liberties, and democracy itself. The "liberal press" has been co-opted. As everyone must know by now, the *New York Times* has totally failed its First Amendment obligations, allowing Judith Miller to make war propaganda for the Bush administration, suppressing for an entire year the news that the Bush administration was illegally spying on American citizens, and denying coverage to Al Gore's speech that challenged the criminal deeds of the Bush administration.

The TV networks mimic Fox News' faux patriotism. Anyone who depends on print, TV, or right-wing talk radio media is totally misinformed. The Bush administration has achieved a de facto Ministry of Propaganda.

The years of illegal spying have given the Bush administration power over the media and the opposition. Journalists and Democratic politicians don't want to have their adulterous affairs broadcast over television or to see their favorite online porn sites revealed in headlines in the local press with their names attached. Only people willing to risk such disclosures can stand up for the country.

Homeland Security and the USA Patriot Act are not our protectors. They undermine our protection by trashing the Constitution and the civil liberties it guarantees. Those with a tyrannical turn of mind have always used fear and hysteria to overcome obstacles to their power and to gain new means of silencing opposition.

Consider the no-fly list. This list has no purpose whatsoever but to harass and disrupt the livelihoods of Bush's critics. If a known terrorist were to show up at check-in, he would be arrested and taken into custody, not told that he could not fly. What sense does it make to tell someone who is not subject to arrest and who has cleared screening that he or she cannot fly? How is this person any more dangerous than any other passenger?

If Senator Ted Kennedy, a famous senator with two assassinated brothers, can be put on a no-fly list, as he was for several weeks, anyone can be put on the list. The list has no accountability. People on the list cannot even find out why they are on the list. There is no recourse, no procedure for correcting mistakes.

I am certain that there are more Bush critics on the list than there are terrorists. According to reports, the list now comprises 80,000 names! This number must greatly dwarf the total number of terrorists in the world and certainly the number of known terrorists.

How long before members of the opposition party, should there be one, find that they cannot return to Washington for important votes, because they have been placed on the no-fly list? What oversight does Congress or a panel of federal judges exercise over the list to make sure there are valid reasons for placing people on the list?

If the government can have a no-fly list, it can have a no-drive list. The Iraqi resistance has demonstrated the destructive potential of car bombs. If we are to believe the government's story about the Murrah Federal Office Building in Oklahoma City, Timothy McVeigh showed that a rental truck bomb could destroy a large office building. Indeed, what is to prevent the government from having a list of people who are not allowed to leave their homes? If the Bush administration can continue its policy of picking up people anywhere in the world and detaining them indefinitely without having to show any evidence for their detention, it can do whatever it wishes.

Many readers have told me, some gleefully, that I will be placed on the no-fly list along with all other outspoken critics of the growth in unaccountable executive power and war based on lies and deception. It is just a matter of time. Unchecked, unaccountable power grows more audacious by the day. As one reader recently wrote, "when the president of the United States can openly brag about being a felon, without fear of the consequences, the game is all but over."

Congress and the media have no fight in them, and neither, apparently, do the American people. Considering the feebleness of the opposition, perhaps the best strategy is for the opposition to shut up, not merely for our own safety but, more importantly, to remove any impediments to Bush administration self-destruction. The sooner the Bush administration realizes its goals of attacking Iran, Syria, and the Shia militias in Lebanon, the more likely the administration will collapse in the maelstrom before it achieves a viable police state. Hamas' victory in the recent Palestinian elections indicates that Muslim outrage over further U.S. aggression in the Middle East has the potential to produce uprisings in Pakistan, Egypt, Jordan, and Saudi Arabia. Not even Karl Rove and Fox News could spin Bush out of the catastrophe.

Perhaps we should go further and join the neocon chorus, urging on invasions of Iran and Syria and sending in the Marines to disarm Hizbullah in Lebanon. Not even plots of the German High Command could get rid of Hitler, but when Hitler marched German armies into Russia he destroyed himself. If Iraq hasn't beat the hubris out of what Gordon Prather aptly terms the "neo-crazies," U.S. military adventures against Iran and Hizbullah will teach humility to the neo-crazies.

Many patriotic readers have written to me expressing their frustration that fact and common sense cannot gain a toehold in a debate guided by hysteria and disinformation. Other readers write that 9/11 shields Bush from accountability.

Debate is dead in America for two reasons: One is that the media concentration permitted in the 1990s has put news and opinion in the hands of a few corporate executives who do not dare risk their broadcasting licenses by getting on the wrong side of government, or their advertising revenues by becoming "controversial." The media follows a safe line and purveys only politically correct information. The other reason is that Americans today are no longer enthralled by debate. They just want to hear what they want to hear. The right-wing, left-wing, and libertarians alike preach to the faithful. Democracy cannot succeed when there is no debate.

Americans need to understand that many interests are using the "war on terror" to achieve *their* agendas. The Federalist Society is using the "war on terror" to achieve its agenda of concentrating power in the executive and packing the Supreme Court to this effect. The neocons are using the war to achieve their agenda of Israeli hegemony in the Middle East. Police agencies are using the war to remove constraints on their powers and to make themselves less accountable. Republicans are using the war to achieve one-party rule—theirs. The Bush administration is using the war to avoid accountability and evade constraints on executive powers. Arms industries, or what President Eisenhower called the "military-industrial complex," are using the war to fatten profits. Terrorism experts are using the war to gain visibility. Security firms are using it to gain customers. Readers can add to this list at will. The lack of debate gives carte blanche to these agendas.

One certainty prevails. Bush is committing America to a path of violence and coercion, and he is getting away with it.

Note: President Obama was elected on a platform of change. But nothing has changed. Obama has intensified the war in Afghanistan and started a new war in Pakistan. The Bush regime's police state measures remain in place.

FEBRUARY 6, 2006

CHAPTER 46

Deficits and Deregulation

THE KEYNESIAN ECONOMISTS, WHO DOMINATED ANGLO-AMERICAN economics in the post-war era, never met a budget deficit that they did not like until Reagan's. All of a sudden budget deficits became a club with which to beat the Reagan administration.

Supply-side economics lowered the value of the human capital of Keynesian economists and displaced them as Washington's policy advisors. The loss of influence infuriated the academic liberals who had used budget deficits, which they had sanctified as a tool for maintaining full employment, to expand the size of government through the growth of federal debt without having to face the taxpayers with legislated increases in tax rates.

What it boiled down to was that budget deficits that resulted from increases in federal government spending were desirable, but not deficits that resulted from across-the-board cuts in marginal tax rates. Cutting tax rates at the upper end was regarded as being outside the bounds of economics. It worsened the income distribution and was an affront to liberal morality. The Keynesian economists did not understand that in the U.S. income is redistributed through the expenditure side of the budget, not through the revenue side. Even a regressive income tax is redistributive if the revenues fund income support programs only for the poor. It is the Bush-Obama bank bailout that redistributes federal revenues to the rich.

President Reagan is criticized for adding $1 trillion to the federal debt during his eight years in office, an amount President Obama added in his first six months. During the Reagan years, the Keynesian economists who had been displaced as policymakers tried to scare Wall Street with "twin deficits" doom and gloom in the hopes that fear would drive up interest rates and wreck the Reagan economy. Harvard University's Benjamin Friedman was one such fear-monger.

It is not unusual today to encounter people who are convinced that Wall Street was the instigator of the Reagan tax rate reductions. However, it was Wall Street economists and publications such as *Barron's* that beat the drums daily about "Reagan's fiscal irresponsibility." Wall Street bought the Keynesian line and expected that Reagan's policy would drive up inflation and interest rates and wreck the stock and bond markets.

Amidst the hullabaloo respected international institutions published data showing that the Reagan deficits ranked low in comparisons with budget deficits of other developed countries. The OECD (Economic Outlook, May 1988) showed that the U.S. budget deficits for 1983–1987 were substantially less as a per centage of GNP/GDP than Canada's, Holland's, Italy's, and Spain's, and on a par with the U.K.'s, Germany's, and France's. None of these countries were regarded as suffering from fiscal irresponsibility.

The Bank for International Settlements showed that the U.S. was not a candidate for "deficit crisis." Between 1973 and 1986 the U.S. experienced one of the lowest growth rates in the ratio of debt to GNP. In the U.S. the ratio rose by 40.8 per cent, but in Germany and Japan, countries that were regarded as hallmarks of fiscal responsibility, the ratio rose 121 per cent and 194 per cent.

The Keynesians ignored all facts. They understood that conservative Republicans were terrified of budget deficits, and they used this fear in their attempt to discredit Reagan's supply-side economics.

Keynesians blamed the deficits on supply-side economists for allegedly predicting that the tax rate reductions would pay for themselves. Keynesians themselves had long been comfortable with their own analysis that showed that tax cuts had a multiplied effect that expanded GNP and brought in more tax revenues. However, the Reagan administration, over whose forecast I had veto power as Assistant Secretary of the Treasury for Economic Policy, made no such forecast. As the official records clearly show, the Reagan administration forecast that every dollar of tax cut would lose a dollar of revenue.

The Reagan deficits, small by today's standard, were the product of two Keynesian concepts: "core inflation" and the "Phillips curve." The "Phillips curve" postulated trade-offs between employment (growth) and inflation. A growing economy would have to pay for its growth by accepting a higher rate of inflation. The price of restraining inflation was a higher rate of unemployment and less economic growth.

These concepts had no credibility with the supply-side and monetarist economists in the Reagan Treasury. However, OMB director David Stockman and the politicians on the White House staff feared that a forecast with budget deficits would lose the Republican vote in Congress and defeat Reagan's attempt to cure "stagflation." Stockman brought the "Phillips curve" into the forecast and used it to raise the projected rates of inflation closer to Keynesian expectations. The higher inflation forecast pushed up nominal GNP and produced the revenues to balance the five-year budget forecast. As I showed in my testimony before the Senate Banking Committee, February 18, 1987, it was the collapse of inflation compared to the forecast that caused the Reagan deficits.

The unexpected collapse of inflation resulted in $2.5 trillion less nominal GNP during 1981–86. The loss of projected tax revenue from lower than projected nominal GNP was the main source of the budget deficits.

Paul Volcker, Federal Reserve chairman at that time, is responsible for the deficits. The Reagan administration asked Volcker to gradually reduce the growth rate of the money supply by 50 per cent over a period of four to six years. Instead, while warning of future inflation from the tax cuts, Volcker collapsed the growth of the money supply and delivered 75 per cent of the requested reduction in 1981. By 1982, inflation was already at the low rate the Reagan administration had predicted for 1986.

All of these facts were available, but Keynesian economists chose to ignore them. Benjamin Friedman even wrote a book in which he claimed that the Reagan administration had purposely engineered large budget deficits in order to force cuts in federal spending. In Keynesian mythology, the Reagan deficits, puny by any measure compared to those of today that Keynesians such as Paul Krugman and Robert Reich regard as "too small," remain the source of all of America's economic ills.

Paul Krugman, who owes his name recognition among the general public in part to his 30-year quarrels with President Reagan and supply-side economics, has even put the blame on the Reagan administration for the Clinton-Bush financial deregulation, which wrecked the financial system, the economy, and Americans' pensions and home values. On occasion I encounter the question from readers: "When are you going to apologize for deregulating the financial system?"

The disinformation spread by people who purport to be scholars is extraordinary. The Reagan administration did not deregulate the financial system. Indeed, we did not even talk about it. The deregulation of the financial system was accomplished by Goldman Sachs and the banks during the Clinton and Bush administrations, after Reagan was gone from the White House and in his grave.

The kind of regulation that concerned the Reagan administration was abusive regulation that was pointless and even devoid of statutory basis. Small businesses were being harassed and threatened with fines by OSHA for not having exit signs over the only door into and out of their offices. Paperwork burdens that provided no benefits commensurate with costs were exploding. On occasion farfetched "violations" resulted in unjust prison sentences. For example, Ocie and Carey Mills, armed with a state permit, used clean dirt to level a building lot. Their action was legal under Florida law. However, federal bureaucrats claimed jurisdiction under the Clean Water Act, which regulates the discharge of pollutants into the "navigable waters of the U.S." No waters, navigable or otherwise, were present, but for putting clean dirt on dry land, father and son spent 21 months in prison.

Mills and his son were imprisoned for a regulatory violation that had no statutory basis. The Clean Water Act makes no reference to wetlands and conveys no powers to the executive branch to create wetlands regulations. This fact was subsequently acknowledged by the Clinton administration, which declared: "Congress should amend the Clean Water Act to make it consistent with the agencies' rule-making."

Similar bureaucratic overreach harassed farmers for cleaning drainage ditches and ranchers for repairing fence posts.

The Reagan administration is sometimes accused of starting financial deregulation by deregulating savings and loan associations. This is nonsense. S & L associations borrowed short and lent long on home mortgages, which comprised their loan portfolios. When short-term interest rates rose above long term-interest rates, the thrifts were victims of disintermediation. Disintermediation prevented Regulation Q from maintaining the spread between the interest paid to depositors and the interest rate on mortgages. The Tax Reform Act of 1986 decreased the value of investments held by S & Ls and worsened balance sheets. The regulatory changes that ensued, some of which were ill-considered, were responses to crisis that developed. They were not the beginning of an onslaught on financial regulation.

Prior to Goldman Sachs taking charge of U.S. financial policy, the only financial deregulation of note was the dismantling of restrictions on national bank branching. This occurred in 1994 and had nothing to do with "Reaganomics." Indeed, I opposed it in my writings, as did real bankers, such as George Champion, the retired chairman of Chase Manhattan Bank, who testified against it in Congress.

Champion's argument was simple. National branch banking would divert banks from their *raison d'être*, which was to identify local business talent and underwrite entrepreneurial efforts in local economies. Champion told the Senate that managers of branches would see their assignments as short-term ones. Consequently, the managers would neglect local needs, instead investing the bank's funds in financial instruments while they waited to move up to a larger branch in a larger town or city. However, large banks wanted national branches as a means of vacuuming up deposits, and they prevailed over common sense.

Liberals and the political left-wing see deregulation as an ideological program of conservatives, of which the Reagan administration was the last political manifestation. Even when Wall Street investment banks, in full view of the public, corrupt the regulatory authorities, the White House, and Congress, liberals blame Reagan. By such self-deception, liberals maintain their faith in government.

CHAPTER 47

The Health Care Deceit

T
HE CURRENT HEALTH CARE "DEBATE" SHOWS HOW FAR GONE representative government is in the United States. Members of Congress represent the powerful interest groups that fill their campaign coffers, not the people who vote for them.

The health care bill is not about health care. It is about protecting and increasing the profits of the insurance companies. The main feature of the health care bill is the "individual mandate," which requires that everyone in America buy health insurance. Senate Finance Committee chairman Max Baucus (D-Mont), a recipient of millions in contributions over his career from the insurance industry, proposes to impose up to a $3,800 fine on Americans who fail to purchase health insurance.

The determination of "our" elected representatives to serve the insurance industry is so compelling that Congress is incapable of recognizing the absurdity of these proposals.

The reason there is a health care crisis in the U.S. is that the cumulative loss of jobs and benefits has swollen the uninsured to approximately 50 million Americans. They cannot afford health insurance any more than employers can afford to provide it.

It is absurd to mandate that people purchase what they cannot afford and to fine them for failing to do so. A person who cannot pay a health insurance premium cannot pay the fine.

These proposals are like solving the homeless problem by requiring the homeless to purchase a house.

In his speech Obama said "we'll provide tax credits" for "those individuals and small businesses who still can't afford the lower-priced insurance available in the exchange" and he said low-cost coverage will be offered to those with preexisting medical conditions. A tax credit is useless to those without income unless the credit is refundable, and subsidized coverage doesn't do much for those millions of Americans with no jobs.

Baucus masquerades as a defender of the health-impaired with his proposal to require insurers to provide coverage to all comers as if the problem of health care can be reduced to preexisting conditions and cancelled policies. It was left to Rep. Dennis Kucinich to point out that the health care bill ponies up 30 million more customers for the private insurance companies.

The private sector is no longer the answer, because the income levels of the vast majority of Americans are insufficient to bear the cost of health insurance today. To provide some perspective, the *monthly* premium for a 60-year-old female for a group policy (employer-provided) with Blue Cross-Blue Shield in Florida is about $1,200. That comes to $14,400 per year. Only employees in high productivity jobs that can provide both a livable salary and health care can expect to have employer-provided coverage. If a 60-year-old female has to buy a non-group policy as an individual, the premium would be even higher. How, for example, is a Wal-Mart shelf stocker or check out clerk going to be able to pay a private insurance premium?

Even the present public option—Medicare—is very expensive to those covered. Basic Medicare is insufficient coverage. Part B has been added, for which about $100 per month is deducted from the covered person's Social Security check. If the person is still earning or has other retirement income, an "income-related monthly adjustment" is also deducted as part of the Part B premium. And if the person is still working, his earnings are subject to the 2.9 per cent Medicare tax.

Even with Part B, Medicare coverage is still insufficient except for the healthy. For many people, additional coverage from private supplementary policies, such as the ones sold by AARP, is necessary. These premiums can be as much as $277 per month. Deductibles remain and prescriptions are only 50 per cent covered. If the drug prescription policy is chosen, the premium is higher.

This leaves a retired person on Medicare who has no other retirement income of significance paying as much as $4,500 per year in premiums in order to create coverage under Medicare that still leaves half of his prescription medicines out-of-pocket. Considering the cost of some prescription medicines, a Medicare-covered person with Part B and a supplementary policy can still face bankruptcy.

Therefore, everyone should take note that a "public option" can leave people with large out-of-pocket costs. I know a professional who has chosen to continue working beyond retirement age. His Medicare coverage with supplemental coverage, Medicare tax, and income-related monthly adjustment comes to $16,400 per year. Those people who want to deny Medicare to the rich will cost the system a lot of money.

What the U.S. needs is a single-payer not-for-profit health system that pays doctors and nurses sufficiently that they will undertake the arduous training and accept the stress and risks of dealing with illness and diseases.

A private health care system worked in the days before expensive medical technology, malpractice suits, high costs of bureaucracy associated with third-party payers and heavy investment in combating fraud, and pressure on insurance companies from Wall Street to improve "shareholder returns."

Despite the rise in premiums, payments to health care providers, such as doctors, appear to be falling along with coverage to policy holders. The system is no longer functional and no longer makes sense. Health care has become an incidental rather than primary purpose of the health care system. Health care plays second fiddle to insurance company profits and salaries to bureaucrats engaged in fraud prevention and discovery. There is no point in denying coverage to one-sixth of the population in the name of saving a nonexistent private free market health care system.

The only way to reduce the cost of health care is to take the profit and paperwork out of health care.

Nothing humans design will be perfect. However, Congress is making it clear to the public that the wrong issues are front and center, such as the concern of Rep. Joe Wilson (R-SC) and others that illegal aliens and abortions will be covered if government pays the bill.

Debate focuses on subsidiary issues, because Congress no longer writes the bills it passes. As Theodore Lowi made clear in his book, *The End of Liberalism*, the New Deal transferred law-making from the legislative to the executive branch. Executive branch agencies and departments write bills that they want and hand them off to sponsors in the House and Senate. Powerful interest groups took up the same practice. The interest groups that finance political campaigns expect their bills to be sponsored and passed.

Thus: a health care reform bill based on forcing people to purchase private health insurance and fining them if they do not.

When bills become mired in ideological conflict, as has happened to the health care bill, something usually passes nevertheless. The president, his PR team, and members of Congress want a health care bill on their resume and to be able to claim that they passed a health care bill, regardless of whether it provides any health care.

The cost of adding public expenditures for health care to a budget drowning in red ink from wars, bank bailouts, and stimulus packages means that the most likely outcome of a health care bill will benefit insurance companies and use mandated private coverage to save public money by curtailing Medicare and Medicaid.

The public's interest is not considered to be the important determinant. The politicians have to please the insurance companies and reduce health care expenditures in order to save money for another decade or two of war in the Middle East.

The telltale part of Obama's speech was the applause in response to his pledge that "I will not sign a plan that adds one dime to our deficits." Yet, Obama and his fellow politicians have no hesitation to add trillions of dollars to the deficit in order to fund wars and to bail out financial gangsters.

The profits of military/security companies are partly recycled into campaign contributions. To cut war spending in order to finance a public health care system would cost politicians campaign contributions from both the insurance industry and the military/security industry.

Politicians are not going to allow that to happen.

It was the war in Afghanistan, not health care, that President Obama declared to be a "necessity."

SEPTEMBER 14, 2009

PART TWO

The War of the Worlds

CHAPTER 48

Where Economics (Mainly) Succeeds

ECONOMICS CAN SUCCESSFULLY EXPLAIN THE EFFICIENT ALLO-
cation of resources by the price system and the allocation of investment by profitability. Relatively speaking, these successes are new.
It was Alfred Marshall at the turn of the 20th century who explained
price formation. Prior to Marshall, economists debated whether price
was determined by the cost of production or by demand—what people
were willing to pay. Marshall ended the controversy by pointing out that
supply and demand are the two blades of the scissors. Together they
determine price.

Profit is the normal return on capital. A normal profit depends on
time and circumstances. It is the profit necessary to retain capital in
an activity. If capital cannot earn a normal rate of return in an activity,
capital is not supplied to that activity. This ensures that capital is not
wasted in low value uses. Whenever capital earns a higher than normal
return, it is a sign that it is employed in a high value use. The excess
profits will lead to an expansion of investment in that use until profits
are reduced to normal.

Without price and profit signals, there is no way of knowing how to
efficiently use resources to produce the highest valued output. The Soviet
economy failed because the system's gross output indicators, the main
signal of managerial and plan success, could not tell if inputs were more
valuable than outputs.

The study of the price system is known as microeconomics. It is the
soundest field of economics. "Free prices" simply means the freedom of
prices to change with supply and demand. It does not mean laissez faire
or no rules and regulations. The "free market" means the freedom of
prices to change as conditions change.

Economists concluded from the Great Depression that a price system
could function without ensuring full employment. This conclusion led

to the rise of macroeconomics, the study of the factors leading to the overall level of prices and employment.

John Maynard Keynes was the first macroeconomist. With his 1936 book, *The General Theory of Employment, Interest and Money*, he spawned the Keynesian economics, of which the American economist Paul Samuelson is doyen. Keynesian macroeconomists concluded that employment and the price level depend on the level of total spending. If consumers saved more than investors invested, it would result in a leakage from the spending stream and a shortage of aggregate demand (the total demand for resources from consumption and investment). The shortfall in spending would cause a decline in employment and prices.

On the other hand, if somehow there was an excess of spending, the demand on resources would drive up prices and the economy would experience inflation.

Macroeconomists concluded that the way to manage the economy was for the government to manage demand. If there was insufficient spending to maintain full employment, the government would fill in the gap by running a deficit in its budget. That is, the government would spend more than it received in tax revenues, thus adding to aggregate demand.

If there was too much spending, the government would reduce the amount by running a budget surplus. In other words, the government would collect more in tax revenues than it would spend, thus contracting the spending stream.

The Keynesians were on to something, but the only economist (a physical chemist actually) who got it right was Michael Polanyi in his 1945 book, *Full Employment and Free Trade* (Cambridge University Press). Polanyi correctly interpreted Keynes' theory to mean that widespread unemployment meant that there was a dearth of money. What the government needed to do was to expand the monetary circulation. It could do this, Polanyi noted, simply by printing money to pay its bills.

Polanyi was on to more important deductions than the Keynesians. He said that it was pointless and expensive for the government to borrow money, on which it had to pay interest, in order to spend, when it could far more cheaply provide the missing purchasing power by printing the money to cover its budget deficit. Polanyi saw fiscal policy as a way to expand the money supply when reluctance or impaired ability to borrow and lend prevented the central bank from expanding the supply of money.

At that time, Polanyi's conclusions were over the head of the economics profession. But two decades later, in the 1960s, Milton Friedman and Anna Schwartz made it clear that the depression in the U.S. during the 1930s was caused by Federal Reserve mistakes that resulted in one-third shrinkage in the supply of money. The depression in the U.K. following World War I resulted from the decision by the British government to go back on the gold standard at the prewar parity of the British pound sterling and gold. As the money supply had expanded so much, the return to gold at prewar parity required shrinkage in the money supply, a shrinkage that collapsed employment and prices.

Thus, the Keynesians, who had the right idea, initially did not understand that full employment was a monetary phenomenon. If government spent more by borrowing to finance its deficit, its borrowing reduced spending on consumption and investment just as taxation did. A budget deficit could boost consumer demand only if the central bank accommodated the deficit by expanding the money supply.

The Keynesians' second mistake came from their failure to understand the impact of fiscal policy on supply. To maintain full employment, the Keynesians came to rely on monetary expansion. Keynesian demand management kept money and credit abundant to ensure sufficient spending. To restrain inflation, Keynesians relied on high tax rates to withdraw spending power from the population that the easy monetary policy provided. The Keynesian economists believed that high taxes served to reduce consumer demand to noninflationary levels. In fact, high tax rates reduced the supply of labor and the supply of goods and services, while easy money pushed up consumer demand. Consequently, prices rose.

The Keynesian demand management policy came unglued during the Carter administration in the late 1970s, when worsening trade-offs between inflation and unemployment left macroeconomists with no policy solution except wage and price controls. In other words, the failure of macroeconomics meant that the price system would not be allowed to allocate resources.

Congress had recently had an experience with fixing one price—the price of oil—and it had been a disaster. Congress was in no mood to fix all prices. Congress preferred to listen to new voices, the voices of "supply-side economists" (in contrast to Keynesian "demand-side economists"). Supply-side economists were new macroeconomists who had both blades of the scissors. They pointed out that, in Keynesian macroeconomics, fiscal policy (changes in tax rates or changes in government spending) only affects aggregate demand: higher taxes reduce consumer purchasing power and total spending declines, lower taxes increase consumer purchasing power and aggregate demand rises. Supply-side economists said that, in fact, changes in marginal tax rates (the rate of tax on additions to income) change aggregate supply.

Supply-side economics is a correction to Keynesian demand management. It has nothing to do with "trickle-down economics" or with a claim that tax cuts pay for themselves. Supply-side economics says that some fiscal policies shift the aggregate supply curve, not the aggregate demand curve. Specifically, if marginal tax rates are raised, there will be fewer goods and services supplied at every price. If marginal tax rates are lowered, there will be more goods and services available at every price.

Today, this conclusion is no longer controversial. But in the 1970s it was a new thought. Initially, Keynesians resisted it, but in the mid-1980s Paul Samuelson came to terms with supply-side economics in the 12th edition of his economics textbook and accepted in principle the relative price effects of fiscal policy.

By bringing relative prices that affect individual behavior into macroeconomics, supply-side economists integrated micro with macroeconomics, a long-standing goal that economics had not achieved. Supply-side economists showed that a shift in marginal tax rates changes relative prices and affects individual decisions whether to save more or to consume more, and whether to work more or to enjoy more leisure. The allocation of income between saving (investment) and consumption and the allocation of time between work and leisure affect the growth rate of the economy. (See Paul Craig Roberts, *The Supply-Side Revolution*, Harvard University Press, 1984.)

Think about it this way: The cost of current consumption is the foregone future income from saving and investment. Income is an after-tax phenomenon. The higher the tax rate on income, the less current consumption costs in terms of foregone future income or, in other words, the less future income is given up by today's consumption. The lower the tax rate, the larger the amount of future income that is lost by consuming instead of investing.

For example, consider the 98 per cent tax rate on investment income that was the rule in England prior to Prime Minister Margaret Thatcher. Suppose a person has £100,000. Shall he invest it or purchase a Rolls Royce? If he invests the money at, say, 10 per cent, he would earn £10,000 before tax. But after-tax, his earnings would be reduced to £200. Thus, the opportunity cost of the Rolls Royce is a measly £200 a year in foregone income. The high tax rate on investment income makes current consumption extremely inexpensive in terms of foregone income.

If the tax rate on investment income is 15 per cent, the cost of the Rolls Royce in terms of foregone income would be 8,500 pounds per year, or 42.5 times as much annually. The 98 per cent tax rate on investment income makes the Rolls Royce essentially a free good. The 15 per cent tax rate makes the car purchase expensive.

Similarly, the cost of leisure is the income given up by not working. The higher the tax rate, the less the after-tax income lost by using time for leisure instead of work. The lower the tax rate, the more expensive is leisure in terms of foregone income. The marginal tax rate on earned income thus affects the supply of labor.

Supply-side economics also corrected a mistake in capital theory. Economists taught that the interest rate determines the cost of capital. If the interest rate is high, capital is costly and investment small. If the interest rate is low, capital is cheap and investment flourishes. At one time this theory made sense, and that time was prior to the income tax. Capital theory originated prior to the income tax, and until supply-side economists came along, no adjustment was made for the impact of taxation on the cost of capital. When there is an income tax, profits or the earnings of capital are an after-tax phenomenon. The higher the tax rates, the higher the cost of capital, and the less is investment and the growth of the economy. (See Paul Craig Roberts, Aldona Robbins, and Gary Robbins, "The Relative Impact of Taxation and Interest Rates on the Cost of Capital," in *Technology and Economic Policy*, edited by Ralph Landau and Dale Jorgenson, 1986.)

Supply-side economists added supply to the macroeconomic scissors. Prior to supply-side economics in the 1970s, macroeconomics was stuck in the pre-Marshallian past. The stagflation that destroyed Jimmy Carter's presidency was induced by policy. Demand-side Keynesians pumped up consumer demand with easy money, while they restrained output with high tax rates. The result was stagflation.

People unfamiliar with facts claim that it was Federal Reserve chairman Paul Volcker's tight monetary policy that cured stagflation. This erroneous claim ignores that prior to the Reagan administration's supply-side policy, tight monetary policy had had no effect on stagflation. Indeed, all Volcker's tight money did was to drive interest rates on money market funds to 17 per cent, thus providing plenty of consumer spending power to drive inflation higher while high tax rates suppressed investment.

Today, Keynesian economics has been reconciled with monetarism and with supply-side economics, making macroeconomics a coherent whole.

However, today macroeconomic policy faces new challenges. In the 21st century, the U.S. economy has been kept going by an expansion in consumer debt, not by rises in consumers' real incomes. Consumers are up to their eyeballs in credit card and mortgage debt. They are no longer in a position to borrow more in order to spend more. Interest rates are very low, and the government's budget deficit is very large; yet, the economy is sinking.

Monetary and fiscal policy cannot help when the problem is that American jobs have been relocated offshore. Because of offshore production, stimulating demand stimulates production in China and other offshore sites. As high-productivity jobs have been offshored, American incomes, except for the super-rich, have ceased to grow. Thus, there is no effective way to boost consumer spending short of printing money and giving it to the population, or handing out tax rebates accommodated by monetary expansion.

Prior to the collapse of world socialism and the rise of the high-speed Internet, it was not possible to offshore jobs or production for U.S. markets to any significant extent. In those prior times, American incomes rose with productivity. If a glitch in employment occurred, an expansionary demand-side or supply-side policy would boost employment and GNP. Today, the jobs have been moved abroad. They are no longer here waiting on an expansionary policy to call Americans back to work.

Trade deficits mean that consumers have spent their money on goods produced abroad at the expense of domestic GDP and employment growth. Writing on the *CounterPunch* website (Dec. 11, 2008), economist Peter Morici reports that U.S. GDP is $1.5 trillion smaller as a result of the record trade deficits accumulated over the last 10 years.

A country that gives away its productive capability and becomes dependent on foreign creditors to finance its budget and trade deficits is a country that has problems beyond the reach of monetary and fiscal policies. For example, no country's borrowing ability is unlimited. The U.S. has been financing its trade and budget deficits by turning over the ownership of existing U.S. assets and their income streams to foreigners and by foreigners recycling their trade surplus dollars into the purchase of new U.S. Treasury debt. This dependence on foreign creditors now constrains U.S. monetary and fiscal policy.

Such creditors hold most of their reserves in dollar-denominated assets. The low interest rates and large budget deficits that are the traditional macroeconomic response to recession make America's creditors reluctant to add to their dollar holdings. The question has risen whether the U.S. can continue to hemorrhage debt and retain the reserve currency role. If the U.S. dollar is dethroned as reserve currency, the U.S. would no longer be able to pay its bills in its own currency. Such a development would complicate America's financing needs. The U.S. is an import-dependent country, dependent on foreigners for energy, manufactured goods, and advanced technology products.

The U.S. has been able to consume more than it produces and to borrow more than it saves because the dollar is the reserve currency. Other countries that get into such a situation either go broke and lose all access to credit or accept an International Monetary Fund austerity program that forces them to curtail consumption and to pay down debt. For the U.S., an IMF austerity program would mean a substantial reduction in living standards.

What can be done? As it would be very difficult for the U.S. to get its house in order if it were to lose the reserve currency role, the government should take immediate action to preserve this role. Preserving the dollar as reserve currency requires large reductions in trade and budget deficits, a tall order for the current weak state of the U.S. economy.

The U.S. can reduce the budget deficit by hundreds of billions of dollars by ending its pointless and illegal wars in the Middle East, by closing hundreds of overseas military bases, and by cutting an overstuffed military budget. This would require the U.S. to give up its goal of world hegemony, but now that America's creditors have seen its aggressiveness, they are unlikely to continue financing U.S. militarism. Better to give up an unrealizable goal than to have it yanked away.

In traditional economic analysis, rising domestic unemployment curtails imports as consumers have less income to spend, thus reducing the trade deficit. The U.S. needs to do much more. U.S. manufacturing has declined so much that, should its creditors permit, the time is not far off when the U.S. trade deficit becomes as large a share of GDP as its manufacturing output.

Offshored production needs to be brought home. When corporations offshore their production for U.S. markets, they reduce U.S. GDP and increase the trade deficit, dollar for dollar.

The U.S. could, perhaps, bring home its offshored production by abolishing the corporate income tax, instead taxing corporations according to the amount of value added to their products that occurs in the U.S. Corporations that produce their products in the U.S. would have a low rate of tax; those that offshore their production would have a high rate of tax.

This change would take time to become effective, and in the near term it could anger creditors, such as China. However, if the policy was seen as credible, the world would see a renewed prospect for the U.S. dollar as reserve currency.

Another helpful reform would be to overthrow performance pay for management based on short-term profits. Quarterly reporting and the cap on executive pay that is not performance based gives U.S. corporations a very short-time horizon compared to overseas competitors.

These suggestions would have to run the gauntlet of ideologies on both the right and the left. Moreover, the hubris of American elites might outlast the window of opportunity that exists for the renewal of the U.S. economy.

CHAPTER 49

Where Economics Fails: The Problem of Free Trade

U NTIL RECENTLY, ECONOMISTS BELIEVED THAT THE CASE FOR free trade was unassailable. Most economists still think that the case is secure, but the two necessary conditions for David Ricardo's 200-year-old theory are no longer present in the modern world. Moreover, the latest work in trade theory, *Global Trade and Conflicting National Interests* (MIT Press, 2000), by Ralph E. Gomory and William J. Baumol, shows that the case for free trade was incorrect from the beginning.

Let's begin with the original case for free trade. It is based on the principle of comparative advantage. This principle says that it pays two countries to specialize and to trade even if one country can produce all tradable goods at a lower cost than the other country. This conclusion follows from countries having different "opportunity costs" of producing tradable goods. The opportunity cost of any good is the other goods that could have been produced by the same resources.

Ricardo uses as examples wine and wool. Portugal can produce both wine and wool cheaper than England, but Portugal has to give up more bottles of wine to gain a yard of woolen cloth than England. Thus, Portugal has a comparative advantage in producing wine, and England has a comparative advantage in producing wool. If each country specializes where it has comparative advantage, the total production of wine and wool will be greater than if each country produced both products. "The gains from trade" result from sharing the increase in total output by trading the two commodities on terms favorable to both countries. Therefore, specialization and trade will allow each country more consumption of both products than if each country were self-sufficient.

The different opportunity costs of one good in terms of another (the cost of wine in terms of wool) means that the trading partners have different relative price ratios for producing tradable goods. It is this difference that creates comparative advantage. In Ricardo's time, unique national characteristics, climate, and geography were important determinants of relative costs. Today, however, most combinations of inputs that produce outputs are knowledge-based. The relative price ratios are the same in every country. Therefore, as opportunity costs do not differ across national boundaries, there is no basis for comparative advantage.

Ricardo's other necessary condition for comparative advantage is that a country's capital seeks its comparative advantage in its home country and does not seek more productive use abroad. Ricardo confronts the possibility that English capital might migrate to Portugal to take advantage of the lower costs of production, thus leaving the English workforce unemployed, or employed in less productive ways. He is able to dismiss this undermining of comparative advantage because of "the difficulty with which capital moves from one country to another" and because capital is insecure "when not under the immediate control of its owner." This insecurity, "fancied or real," together "with the natural disinclination which every man has to quit the country of his birth and connections, and entrust himself, with all his habits fixed, to a strange government and new laws, check the emigration of capital. These feelings, which I should be sorry to see weakened, induce most men of property to be satisfied with a low rate of profits in their own country, rather than seek a more advantageous employment for their wealth in foreign lands."

Today, these feelings have been weakened. Men of property have been replaced by corporations. Once the large excess supplies of Asian labor were available to American corporations, once Congress limited the tax deductibility of CEO pay that was not "performance related," once Wall Street pressured corporations for higher shareholder returns, once Wal-Mart ordered its suppliers to meet "the Chinese price," once hostile takeovers could be justified as improving shareholder returns by offshoring production, capital departed the country.

Today capital is as mobile as traded goods. Indeed, capital can move with the speed of light, but traded goods have to move by ship or airplane. Economists would be hard-pressed to produce stories of American capital seeking comparative advantage in the 50 states. But they can easily show its flight abroad. Approximately half of U.S. imports from China are the offshored production of U.S. firms for the U.S. market.

Most economists, whom I have labeled "no-think economists," learned in graduate school that to question free trade was to be a protectionist—a designation that could harm one's career. I personally know many economists who are terrified to be anything but free traders, but who have no understanding of the theory on which free trade is based or of the theory's many problems.

For most economists, free trade is a dictum like the Bush regime's dictum that Saddam Hussein had "weapons of mass destruction." The six-year, $3 trillion war was pointless, just as is the deindustrializing of the United States by free trade.

I am not the only economist who takes issue with the free-trade dogma. A number of competent economists have taken free-trade theory to the cleaners. For example: Herman E. Daly and John B. Cobb show the inadequacies of the theory in *For the Common Good* (1989). James K. Galbraith puts the theory to rest in *The Predator State* (2008). Robert E. Prasch, in a 1996 article in the *Review of Political Economy*, demonstrates fundamental problems with the theory. Ron Baiman at DePaul University has shown that Ricardo's theory is "mathematically overdetermined and therefore generally unsolvable." Economist Ian Fletcher demonstrates "Fatal Flaws in the Theory of Comparative Advantage" in a November 6, 2008 *American Economic Alert*. In 2004, America's most famous economist, Paul Samuelson, wrote that an improvement in the productivity of one country can decrease the living standard of another. Thus, when U.S. corporations take their technology abroad and integrate it into the productive capability of a foreign country, they reduce the living standards in their home country.

This brings us to Gomory and Baumol. Samuelson's 2004 article is a defense of the powerful new work in trade theory by these two authors. Gomory, one of America's most distinguished mathematicians, and Baumol, a past president of the American Economics Association, show that free-trade theory has many problems because "the modern free-trade world is so different from the original historical setting of the free-trade models."

Gomory and Baumol dismiss the alleged gains from offshoring production for home markets: "In almost all cases, most of the economic benefit stays where the value is added. Profits are usually only a small portion of the value added through economic activity, and most of the value added, such as wages, remains local. It matters to a country to be the site of an economic activity, whoever may own the company."

Gomory and Baumol show that unlike Ricardo's win-win outcome, based on a simple arithmetical example, sophisticated mathematics proves that in most cases "the outcome [from trade] that is best for one country tends not to be good for another." Gomory and Baumol re-establish the gains from trade (win-win situation) as a special case of limited applicability.

The authors conclude that "free trade between nations is not always and automatically beneficial. It can yield many stable equilibria in which a country is worse off than it would be if it isolated itself from trade altogether."

It will take the economics profession 20 years to come to terms with this new work. The myth that America's economic success is based on free trade will be hard to dislodge.

R.W. Thompson, in his *History of Protective Tariff Laws* (1888), showed that protectionism is the father of economic development. Free trade has become an ideology. It once had a Ricardian basis, a basis no longer present in the real world. In the United States of America today, "free trade" is a shield for greed. Short-term gains for management and shareholders are maximized at the expense of the labor force and the economic welfare of the country. Free trade ideology is dismantling the ladders of upward mobility that made America an opportunity society.

CHAPTER 50

Is Offshoring Trade?

O FFSHORING'S PROPONENTS DEFEND THE PRACTICE ON THE grounds that it is free trade and thereby beneficial.

We saw in the previous chapter that free trade is not necessarily beneficial. Let's now examine whether offshoring is trade.

In the traditional Ricardian free trade model, trade results from countries specializing in activities where they have comparative advantage and trading these products for the products of other countries doing likewise. In Ricardo's example, England specializes in woolen cloth and trades wool to Portugal, which specializes in wine, for wine.

In the Ricardian model, trade is not competitive. English wool is not competing against Portuguese wool, and Portuguese wine is not competing against English wine.

Somewhere along the historical way, free trade became identified with competition between countries producing the same products. American TV sets vs. Japanese TV sets. American cars vs. Japanese cars. This meaning of free trade diverged from the Ricardian meaning based on comparative advantage and came to mean innovation and improvements in design and performance driven by foreign competition. Free trade became divorced from comparative advantage without a new theoretical basis being built upon which to base the free trade doctrine.

Countries competing against one another in an array of products and services is not covered by Ricardian trade theory.

Offshoring doesn't fit the Ricardian or the competitive idea of free trade. In fact, offshoring is not trade.

Offshoring is the practice of a firm relocating its production of goods or services for its home market to a foreign country. When a firm moves production offshore, U.S. GDP declines by the amount of the offshored production, and foreign GDP increases by that amount. Employment and consumer income decline in the U.S. and rise abroad. The U.S. tax base shrinks, resulting in reductions in public services or higher taxes or higher interest payments to service deficit spending and the switch to bond finance from tax finance.

When the offshored production comes back to the U.S. to be marketed, the U.S. trade deficit increases dollar for dollar. The trade deficit is financed by turning over to foreigners U.S. assets and their future income streams. Profits, dividends, interest, capital gains, rents, and tolls from leased toll roads now flow from American pockets to foreign pockets, thus worsening the current account deficit as well.

Who benefits from these income losses suffered by Americans? Clearly, the foreign country to which the production is moved. The other prominent beneficiaries are the shareholders and the executives of the companies that offshore production. The lower labor costs raise profits, the share price, and the "performance bonuses" of management.

Offshoring's proponents claim that the lost incomes from job losses are offset by benefits to consumers from lower prices. Yet, they are unable to cite studies that support this claim. The claim is based on the unexamined assumption that offshoring is free trade and, thereby, mutually beneficial.

Proponents also claim that the Americans who are left unemployed soon find equal or better jobs. This claim is based on the assumption that the demand for labor ensures full employment, and that people whose jobs have been moved abroad can be retrained for new equal or better jobs.

These claims are far fetched. Offshoring affects all tradable goods and services. As I have reported on numerous occasions, the nonfarm payroll data collected by BLS makes clear that in the 21st century the U.S. economy has been able to create net new jobs only in nontradeable domestic services, employment that is lowly paid compared to high value-added manufacturing jobs and professional services such as engineering.

Moreover, even services of school teachers and nurses, which cannot be offshored, can, and are, being performed by foreigners brought in on work visas.

The growing number of displaced and discouraged unemployed Americans comprises an external cost inflicted by firms on taxpayers and on the viability of the American political and economic system.

Some offshoring apologists go so far as to imply, and others even to claim, that offshore outsourcing is offset by "insourcing." For example, they point out that the Japanese have built car plants in the U.S. This is a false analogy. The Japanese car plants in the U.S. are an example of direct foreign investment. The Japanese produce in the U.S. in order to sell here. The plants are a response to Reagan era import quotas on Japanese cars and to high transport costs. The Japanese are not producing cars in the U.S. for the purpose of sending them back to Japan to be marketed. They are not using cheaper American labor to produce for the Japanese home market.

Other apologists imply that H-1B and other work visas are a form of "insourcing." They argue that the ability of U.S. firms to bring in foreigners to compensate for alleged shortages of U.S. workers allows the corporations to keep their operations in America and not have to move them abroad. This false claim, which a *Washington Post* editorial (March 2, 2009) endorsed, was rebutted by Senators Charles Grassley and Bernie Sanders, who observed that "with many thousands of financial services workers unemployed, it's absurd to claim that banks can't find top-notch American workers to perform these jobs" (*Washington Post*, March 5, 2009).

The senators could have made a stronger point. The work visa program is supposed to be for specialized, high-tech skills that allegedly are in short-supply in the U.S. In fact, the vast majority of those brought in on work visas are brought in as lower-paid replacements for American workers, who are dismissed after being forced to train their foreign replacements.

The practice of replacing American employees with foreigners brought in on work visas is reported more at the state and local level than nationally. For example, on March 30, 2009, a Charlotte, N.C., TV station, WSOC, reported that Wachovia is cutting labor costs by bringing in foreign replacements for American employees.

Congress forbade banks that receive bailout money from hiring foreigners to replace American employees. But the H-1B lobby got its hands on the legislation and inserted a loophole. The banks cannot directly hire foreigners as replacements for U.S. employees, but they can hire contractors to supply "contract labor." The bank pays the contractor, and the contractor pays the workers.

Computerworld (February 24, 2009) reports that the H-1B visas are becoming the property of Indian contract labor firms, such as Tata, Infosys, Wipro, and Satyam.

These firms contract with American employers to supply reduced-cost labor from abroad with which to replace American employees.

The combination of offshoring and work visas is creating a new kind of American unemployment that cannot be cured by boosting consumer demand. *Business Week* (March 9, 2009) reports that JP Morgan-Chase is increasing its outsourcing to India by 25 per cent. *Computerworld* (February 24, 2009) reports that Nielsen Company, which measures TV audiences and consumer trends for clients, is laying off American employees at a Florida facility after announcing a 10-year global outsourcing agreement valued at $1.2 billion with Tata. *Computerworld* quotes Janice Miller, a city councilwoman: "they are still bringing in Indians, and there are a lot of local people out of work."

The *New York Times* (March 6, 2009) reports that IBM is laying off U.S. employees piecemeal in order to avoid compliance with layoff notice laws. According to the *New York Times*, "IBM's American employment has declined steadily, down to 29 per cent of its worldwide payroll."

The American population is being divorced from the production of the goods and services that they consume. It is the plight of a Third World country to be dependent on goods and services that are not produced by its work force. The unaddressed question is how can Americans employed in domestic services or unemployed purchase the foreign made goods and services that are marketed to them?

If news reports are correct, even the lowest level American jobs are subject to outsourcing. The fast food chain, McDonald's, is experimenting with having drive-up window orders routed to India via a VoIP internet connection. The person in India then posts the order to the kitchen and sends the billing to the cashier. If this works for McDonald's, the laid-off software engineers, IT workers, and former bank employees will not even be able to get a job at a fast food restaurant.

Indeed, Americans already experience difficulty in finding restaurant jobs because of "insourcing." Young people from abroad are brought in on R-1 visas and supplied by contractors to restaurants where they wait tables and do food prep work. In pharmacies, they serve as assistants.

Mexicans have a large share of construction jobs. Americans are finding occupation after occupation closed to them. Free market ideologues justify the destruction of the prospects of millions of Americans as "an increase in the general welfare."

The United States is unable to deal with its serious economic problems, because powerful interest groups benefit from the continuation of the problems. As long as narrow private interests can cloak themselves in free trade's claim of increased general welfare, the American economy will continue its relative and absolute decline, and American taxpayers will continue to bear the cost of workers displaced by offshoring and work visas.

CHAPTER 51

Economics for a Full World

HE FIRST THREE CHAPTERS IN PART TWO DEAL WITH ECONOMICS within the existing paradigm. This chapter deals with the economics that is omitted from the paradigm. The omitted economics is so important that the omission indicates the need for a new paradigm.

The basic problem is that economics does not measure all the costs, and the omitted costs might be the most important costs. Since economics does not measure all the costs, economists cannot know whether growth is economic or uneconomic. The economist Herman Daly, for example, asks if the ecological and social costs of growth have grown larger than the value of the increase in production.

The costs that are left out of the computation of Gross Domestic Product are the depletion of natural capital, such as oil and mineral resources and fisheries, and the pollution of air, water, and land resources.

Economists do a poor job of adjusting economic theory to developments brought by the passage of time. Just as capital theory originated prior to the income tax and free-trade theory originated at a period in history when capital was internationally immobile and tradable goods were based on climate and knowledge differences, economists' neglect of the ecosystem as a finite, entropic, non-growing, and materially-closed system dates from an earlier "empty world."

In an empty world, man-made capital is scarce and nature's capital is plentiful. In an empty world, the fish catch is limited by the number of fishing boats, not by the remaining fish population, and petroleum energy is limited by drilling capability, not by geological deposits. Empty-world economics focuses on the sustainability of man-made capital, not on natural capital. Natural capital is treated as a free good. Using it up is not treated as a cost but as an increase in output.

Economic theory is based on "empty-world" economics. But, in fact, today the world is full. In a "full world," the fish catch is limited by the remaining population of fish, not by the number of fishing boats, which are man-made capital in excess supply. Oil energy is limited by geological deposits, not by the drilling and pumping capacity of man-made capital. In national income accounting, the use of man-made capital is depreciated, but the use of nature's capital has no cost other than extraction cost. Therefore, the using up of natural capital always results in economic growth.

For example, the dead zones in the Gulf of Mexico from fertilizer runoff from chemical fertilizer farming are not counted as a cost against the increase in agricultural output from chemical farming. The brown clouds that reduce light over large areas of Asia are not included as costs in the production of energy from coal. Economists continue to assume that the only limits to growth are labor, man-made capital, and consumer demand. In fact, the critical limit is ecological.

Nature's resources cannot be replicated or regenerated like man-made capital. These real limits to growth are both neglected and denied by economic theory.

Modern economics is based on a "production function," associated with Robert Solow and Joseph Stiglitz, two Nobel prizewinners. A production function explains the relationship between inputs and outputs. The Solow-Stiglitz production function assumes that man-made capital is a substitute for nature's capital. Therefore, as long as man-made capital can be reproduced, there are no limits to growth. As the economists James Tobin (another Nobel prize winner) and William Nordhaus put it in 1972, the implicit assumption is that "reproducible [man-made] capital is a near perfect substitute for land and other exhaustible resources."

Nicholas Georgescu-Roegen, one of the world's most distinguished mathematical economists (now deceased), destroyed the Solow-Stiglitz production function, dismissing it as a "conjuring trick," but economists have nonetheless kept this production function close to their chests, because it is a mathematical way of saying that ecological limits on economic growth do not exist. Nature has no role in the game. (See Herman Daly, *Ecological Economics and Sustainable Development*, U.K.: Edward Elgar Publishing, 2007.)

Modern economics has turned economic growth into an ideology, just as free trade has become an ideology. The Solow-Stiglitz production function is a false explanation of how inputs produce outputs. In contrast with Solow-Stiglitz, Georgescu-Roegen made it clear that production is the transformation of resources into useful products and into waste products. Labor and man-made capital are agents of transformation, while natural resources are what are transformed into useful products and waste products. Man-made capital and natural capital are complements, not substitutes. The Solow-Stiglitz production function, the basis of modern economics, is fantasy.

The real question is whether the world's remaining natural resources and the "sinks" for waste products are sufficient to sustain the continuation of economic growth as traditionally understood and its expansion to underdeveloped countries.

Environmentalists and ecological economists are aware that today the limits to growth include the natural environment. Even politicians are aware, as they have imposed laws and regulations designed to limit pollution.

Over the course of American history, economic growth has made income inequality acceptable, because economic growth, as President Kennedy put it, is "a tide that lifts all boats." What becomes of a society based on the rise in real incomes when ecology imposes its limits? Can statistics forever disguise that the costs outweigh the benefits?

Can a society based on children doing better economically than their parents survive when policy mistakes together with ecological limits disrupt this traditional outcome?

There are social costs associated with the failure of economics to account for the full costs of production and with the integration of all countries into a "global economy." For many countries, being integrated into the global economy means that the society loses control over itself. Entire occupations and ways of life are wiped away as specific countries are forced to forego diversification and to specialize in the products that globalism dictates, regardless of the needs and wants of the domestic population.

Economic globalism is far in advance of global government. As Herman Daly writes, globalism is the "space into which transnational corporations move to escape regulation by national governments." Economic globalism in the absence of global government permits transnational corporations to escape accountability.

This means that today corporations are escaping accountability for costs that they impose on the rest of the world. If these "externalized" costs were included in their cost of production, would there be any basis for CEOs to be paid 300, 400, or 500 times the pay of a production employee?

If ecology imposes limits on growth, ladders of upward mobility cease to function. How would society distribute income in order to ensure social peace? This new distribution would certainly require the end of the current large differences, but would people be locked into place, requiring luck and extraordinary ability to rise?

It is possible that some new plague, natural or man-made, will resurrect an empty world, a world empty as well of natural capital. Just as plague destroyed the Mongol Empire, plague could destroy science and technology, making it difficult for humanity to recover economically from depleted and hard-to-reach natural resources.

In the founding days of the discipline of economics, Adam Smith and Alfred Marshall endeavored to explain reality in order that policy might improve the human condition. Whether they succeeded or failed, they were sincere.

Today, economists play games with assumptions and equations. Smith and Marshall were interested in truth and its discovery. Economists today are interested in money, and they provide apologies for "globalism" that bring grants to their departments from transnational corporations. Today a person who speaks economic truth has no future in the economics department of a university dependent on outside money.

If economics is to serve humankind, the limits imposed by ecological resources must be acknowledged. At a minimum, this requires junking the Solow-Stiglitz production function and substituting that of Georgescu-Roegen. Externalities are not very important in an "empty world," but in a "full world" ignored externalities can offset the value of increased output. When the last species is gone, how is it replenished? How are exhausted oil and mineral deposits refilled? How are destroyed rain forests replanted? How are polluted air, water, and oceans reclaimed?

Unless one believes in science fiction, the answer to these questions is only through the passage of time, in some cases millions of years. To treat resources created by nature over millions of years as devoid of costs, other than the costs of extraction, is absurd. If economics is to be of any use to humanity, it must cease being absurd.

CHAPTER 52

How Real Estate Developers Get Rich by Imposing Costs on Others

"Not Caesar now, but money, is all."—Alain of Lille

HALF A CENTURY AGO, IN HIS BOOK, *The Federal Bulldozer*, Martin Anderson pointed out that urban renewal was a means for liberals to gentrify their cities with federal money at the expense of ethnic neighborhoods and housing for the poor. Anderson was right, but federal spending programs had acquired a moral status that protected them from inconvenient facts. Indeed, today the right of developers to profit by imposing costs on others is more sacrosanct than the Bill of Rights.

In 2009, a developer, in Dawson County, Georgia, succeeded in getting the Dawsonville City Council to rezone 150 acres of rural residential land as commercial/industrial. The developer intends to construct a motorsports race track amid horse farms, wildlife management areas, and low density residential use. The maneuvering began with Dawsonville annexing the land, thus preventing the county from protecting the property owners who invested in a tranquil way of life that the developer and obedient city council have conspired to destroy.

Everyone believes that money changed hands, but no news reporter would dare to investigate.

The developer's profits and the tax revenues he has promised the small town of Dawsonville will not reflect the heavy costs his project imposes on residents in an environment where property values depend on natural beauty and peace and quiet.

In economic jargon, the developer is generating external costs that do not factor into his assessment of the value of his project. The costs are external to the project, because they are imposed on others. The project assigns no value to the quality of life that it destroys.

A fair-minded person would say that the developer should not be allowed to proceed unless he compensates those whose tranquility his project disrupts and whose property values it harms. Many economists, however, especially free market ideologues, will say that if the residents do not want the project they should pay the developer the present value of his expected profits not to go forward with the project.

Obviously, a policy of buying off the developer would bring in another with an even more outrageous project in order to extract higher blackmail.

For free market economists, the property rights *of the developer* are sacrosanct. The property rights of existing owners in tranquility, low density, unobstructed views, and clean air don't count. These rights can be violated at will.

Zoning is society's way of protecting property investments from reclassification that would harm their values. But it has proven an unreliable instrument as developers usually prevail over communities. The Dawsonville City Council changed the rules after residents had made their commitments and after the area had developed in keeping with the original zoning. Such zoning changes, if permitted at all, should be illegal without a two-thirds or three-fourths vote of the residents.

Free market ideologues are opposed to zoning because it protects existing commitments by limiting the rights of a new entrant. Free market ideologues believe that a person has the right to establish a pig farm in the middle of a residential neighborhood or a porn shop next to a church or a half-way house next to an elementary school. Otherwise, the state is interfering with property rights, which means that land is not being put to its most valued use as measured by the profits of the project, profits that are not offset by the costs the project imposes externally on others.

Developers are notorious for imposing high costs on taxpayers. Some local jurisdictions now require developers to put in curbs, sidewalks, water, and sewage. However, many costs of development projects are still passed on to taxpayers.

Consider Walton County in the Florida panhandle, for example. Federal Reserve chairman Alan Greenspan's unrealistic low interest rates and environmentalists, carping about St. Joe's paper mill caused the company to put its vast land holdings into real estate development. The paper company owned miles of undeveloped land along the Gulf coast and hundreds of thousands of acres inland. These vast holdings that had provided pulp wood for the paper mill were filled with vacation homes and shopping centers.

In less than a decade density has increased to the degree that hurricane evacuation is impossible. Taxpayers were shouldered with the cost of turning two-lane roads into four-lane roads and two-lane bridges into four-lane bridges, eventually reaching Interstate-10 70 miles away. Even if St. Joe had been required to pay this cost, the homes and businesses and small towns along the two-lane highway are forever destroyed. A way of life is gone forever, and no one was compensated.

On the national level, financial interests, the military/security complex, and AIPAC rule. On the state and local level real estate developers rule. This is especially the case in Florida where campaign contributions insure that city and county commissions will approve development plans that destroy the natural environment and local communities.

The destruction of Florida by real estate developers is now so extreme that aroused residents have organized an initiative for the November 2010 ballot known as Florida Hometown Democracy. The initiative would require all approved changes in growth plans to be decided by voters in referendums in the affected communities. The real estate lobby is using a campaign of disinformation to fight this effort to curtail its ability to externalize its costs.

Little doubt that economists will rail against Florida Hometown Democracy as an interference with private property rights that will divert land resources "from their most productive use." Floridians need to keep in mind that economists measure "most productive use" by profits that are created by imposing costs of the projects on those who suffer from them. If the full costs were imposed on the projects, few would be undertaken.

Real estate developers are infamous for naming their "developments" after the vistas they destroy. "Oak Hill," for example, will be a hillside subdivision where a forest of oaks once stood. "Walnut Mill Run" memorializes the swift running stream that is now encased in galvanized pipe buried in the backyards of the houses built on the site.

It is easy to beat up real estate developers for their destruction of natural habitat, but they are not the worst generators of external costs. I cannot say which profit-making entity deserves that crown. Externalities generated by the high-density factory farming of meat and eggs might prove to be the most dangerous to humans.

American farm soils are depleted, and crops now depend on chemical fertilizers, the run-off from which destroys water resources. But the factory farming of animals produces dangerous viruses, such as the H1N1 swine flu virus, which first emerged in the late 1980s from intensive pork production in North Carolina and is now, according to some, threatening the world from a subsidiary of Smithfield Farms in Mexico.

The meat that Americans eat is produced in the most inhumane conditions imaginable. No science fiction could do the production process justice. The animals exist in dangerous germ pools in such deplorable conditions that they must be pumped full of antibiotics. I know people who are not vegetarians who refuse to eat meat because of the inhumane, "low-cost" conditions in which it is produced.

The same goes for the production of eggs. There is little doubt that the bird flu virus is a product of the inhumane conditions under which "low-cost" protein is produced.

The "low-cost" production of pork does not include the deaths and illnesses, and the expense of treatment and lost incomes and grief to families, of swine flu.

If there were any justice in America, the corporations whose "low-cost" production methods gave humanity the swine flu would be destroyed in liability lawsuits.

Unfortunately in America, economists believe that "low-cost" production is the be-all and end-all of "consumer satisfaction." Until economists, or preferably people in society, realize that in economic jargon "low-cost" production means maximum external costs imposed on society and the environment, the vaunted unregulated market economy will continue on its path toward the destruction of life on earth.

CHAPTER 53

The Need for Planning

I N THEIR BOOK, *Ecological Economics: Principles and Applications*, Herman Daly and J. Farley point out that in the 20th century both the Soviet Union and the U.S. had economic growth as their first priority. In the Soviet Union, Marx's "new socialist man" would appear only with the disappearance of scarcity, which required the maximum growth in output. In the U.S. high growth was the way to avoid class conflict by producing a larger pie to divide.

Despite their vaunted mathematics, economists have failed to understand that infinite growth in a finite system is impossible. The Soviet economy failed first, because its gross output indicator was more inefficient than the price and profit indicators used in the West.

The West saw Soviet economic failure as proof of market capitalism's superiority. This conclusion was correct up to a point, but the "end of history" euphoria neglected the real end of history implicit in the exhaustion of environmental capital.

For organized human society to deal with the consequences of this exhaustion, planning is essential. But planning is discredited by Soviet failure.

Fortunately, the planning required bears no resemblance to Soviet planning, which was ideological in origin. As I proved in my book, *Alienation and the Soviet Economy* (1971, 1990), the purpose of Soviet planning was to totally eliminate the market and the price and profit signals upon which it relies, and to organize the entire economy as if it were a self-sufficient farm producing for its own use. In a modern economy with large numbers of input and output combinations, this is a strict impossibility.

This is not the kind of planning needed to stave off societal collapse from environmental exhaustion.

As was explained earlier, external costs are not that important in an empty world. But in a full world they may be determining. If external costs were included, many projects today would not get off the ground. Moreover, if economic growth included the external costs of environmental exhaustion, it might not pay.

In 2006 Dmitry Orlov compared the Soviet economic collapse with the coming U.S. economic collapse and concluded that the Soviets were better positioned to survive the economic collapse.

For example, the U.S. is massively dependent on depleting water and energy resources, especially petroleum energy in which it is not self-sufficient. Russia is an exporter of energy. Russia was not dependent on a car economy. Russians could meet their occupational and shopping needs with public transportation. Occupants of Russian housing, as bad as it was, were not subject to mortgage foreclosures and homelessness.

Russians were inured to hardships and accustomed to bartering for their needs. Russian families tended to be in the same place and supportive. U.S. families are widely scattered and less able to come to one another's help.

Despite the notorious failure of Soviet agriculture, basic foodstuffs—cabbages, onions, potatoes—were close at hand. Even many residents of cities had access to garden plots. Even the largest metropolitan areas had surrounding agricultural areas. In the U.S., food is trucked in from vast distances. Garden plots are rare outside of rural areas.

Soviet medicine focused on prevention with immunization programs, infectious disease control, and basic care. The state run clinics and hospitals were not profit-based. In the U.S., health care is a profit system in which doctors refuse to diagnose, instead ordering expensive tests in order to protect themselves against liability claims. If profits leave the system, financing collapses.

My summary barely does justice to Orlov. But the point comes across. The U.S., unlike the Soviet Union, is import-dependent for energy and manufactured goods. Americans are dependent on private cars for access to their jobs, food, and medical care. A disruption in gasoline supply automatically disrupts food deliveries to stores and the ability of the work force to show up for work. Americans are not inured to hardship and lack survival skills.

The development pattern of the U.S. was based on abundant and cheap gasoline. Urban areas became huge metropolitan areas of suburban sprawl, with people traveling large distances on a daily basis in order to earn their keep and to meet their needs.

Surplus U.S. food stocks that were the products of agricultural subsidy programs have been eliminated. Agriculture is increasingly concentrated in large factory farms, whether for grains or meat. Even dairy farms are falling into concentrated hands. Food output is increasingly centralized in locations distant from most cities. A transportation disruption will disrupt food distribution.

While there is time, the U.S. should give thought to the energy implications of suburban development, perhaps subsidize, if necessary, food production near population concentrations, require development plans to specify the water resources, create public transportation systems that can be run by renewable energy, and otherwise prepare itself for both the exhaustion of nature's resources and of the U.S. dollar as world reserve currency. If the future is left to take care of itself, organized society in the U.S. could fail.

The problem with planning is not only government inefficiency, but also the power of organized interest groups to use planning to elevate their interests above those of society. Much thought would have to be given to preventing planning from becoming just another tool of interest groups. Perhaps giving key roles to bodies of independent experts and scientists could mitigate the political corruption, assuming there are still any experts and scientists who are independent and not corruptible.

There is no doubt that the efforts of humans, being imperfect creatures, to plan for life in a full world would be beset with errors and miscalculations. But however imperfect the product would be, the result would be better than what would result from the economists' assumption that man-made capital is a perfect substitute for nature's capital and that, therefore, resources are inexhaustible. To conclude that our future is a continuation of the past is a death warrant for U.S. society.

Index

AK Press

Ordering Information

AK Press
674-A 23rd Street
Oakland, CA 94612-1163
U.S.A
(510) 208-1700
www.akpress.org
akpress@akpress.org

AK Press
PO Box 12766
Edinburgh, EH8 9YE
Scotland
(0131) 555-5165
www.akuk.com
ak@akedin.demon.uk

The addresses above would be delighted to provide you with the latest complete AK catalog, featuring several thousand books, pamphlets, zines, audio products, video products, and stylish apparel published & distributed by AK Press. Alternatively, check out our websites for the complete catalog, latest news and updates, events, and secure ordering.

Also Available from AK Press

The first audio collection from Alexander Cockburn on compact disc.

Beating the Devil

Alexander Cockburn, ISBN 13: 9781902593494 • CD • $14.98

In this collection of recent talks, maverick commentator Alexander Cockburn defiles subjects ranging from Colombia to the American presidency to the Missile Defense System. Whether he's skewering the fallacies of the war on drugs or illuminating the dark crevices of secret government, his erudite and extemporaneous style warms the hearts of even the stodgiest cynics of the left.

Available from CounterPunch/AK Press

Call 1-800-840-3683 or order online from
www.counterpunch.org or www.akpress.org

The Case Against Israel
by Michael Neumann
Wielding a buzzsaw of logic, Professor Neumann dismantles plank-by-plank the Zionist
rationale for Israel as religious state entitled to trample upon the basic human rights of
non-Jews. Along the way, Neumann also offers a passionate amicus brief for the plight of
the Palestinian people.

Other Lands Have Dreams: From Baghdad to Pekin Prison
by Kathy Kelly
At a moment when so many despairing peace activists have thrown in the towel, Kathy
Kelly, a witness to some of history's worst crimes, never relinquishes hope. Other Lands
Have Dreams is literary testimony of the highest order, vividly recording the secret casualties of our era, from the hundreds of thousands of Iraqi children inhumanely denied basic
medical care, clean water and food by the U.S. overlords to young mothers sealed inside the
sterile dungeons of American prisons in the name of the merciless war on drugs.

Dime's Worth of Difference: Beyond the Lesser of Two Evils
Edited by Alexander Cockburn and Jeffrey St. Clair
Everything you wanted to know about one-party rule in America.

Whiteout: the CIA, Drugs and the Press
by Alexander Cockburn and Jeffrey St. Clair, Verso.
The involvement of the CIA with drug traffickers is a story that has slouched into the
limelight every decade or so since the creation of the Agency. In Whiteout, here at last is
the full saga.

Been Brown So Long It Looked Like Green to Me: the Politics of Nature
by Jeffrey St. Clair, Common Courage Press.
Covering everything from toxics to electric power plays, St. Clair draws a savage profile of
how money and power determine the state of our environment, gives a vivid account of
where the environment stands today and what to do about it.

Imperial Crusades: Iraq, Afghanistan and Yugoslavia
by Alexander Cockburn and Jeffrey St. Clair, Verso.
A chronicle of the lies that are now returning each and every day to haunt the deceivers
in Washington and London, the secret agendas and the underreported carnage of these
wars. We were right and they were wrong, and this book proves the case. Never leave home
without it.

Why We Publish CounterPunch

By Alexander Cockburn and Jeffrey St. Clair

TEN YEARS AGO WE FELT UNHAPPY ABOUT THE STATE OF RADICAL JOURNALISM. It didn't have much edge. It didn't have many facts. It was politically timid. It was dull. *CounterPunch* was founded. We wanted it to be the best muckraking newsletter in the country. We wanted it to take aim at the consensus of received wisdom about what can and cannot be reported. We wanted to give our readers a political roadmap they could trust.

A decade later we stand firm on these same beliefs and hopes. We think we've restored honor to muckraking journalism in the tradition of our favorite radical pamphleteers: Edward Abbey, Peter Maurin and Ammon Hennacy, Appeal to Reason, Jacques René Hébert, Tom Paine and John Lilburne.

Every two weeks *CounterPunch* gives you jaw-dropping exposés on: Congress and lobbyists; the environment; labor; the National Security State.

"*CounterPunch* kicks through the floorboards of lies and gets to the foundation of what is really going on in this country", says Michael Ratner, attorney at the Center for Constitutional Rights. "At our house, we fight over who gets to read *CounterPunch* first. Each issue is like spring after a cold, dark winter."

YOU CANNOT MISS ANOTHER ISSUE

Name _____

Address _____

City _____ State _____ Zip _____

Email _____ Phone _____

Credit Card # _____

Exp. Date _____ Signature _____

☐ 1 year **$45**　　☐ 2 year **$80**　　☐ Donation Any Amount

☐ 1 year email **$35**　　☐ 2 year email **$65**　　☐ Low-income/student/senior **$35**

☐ 1 year both **$50**　　☐ 2 year both **$90**　　☐ Low-income/student/senior email **$30**

A one year subscription consists of 22 issues. The email version is a PDF emailed to the email address you include. Please notify CounterPunch of email and mailing address changes. Low-income/student/senior subscriptions are 1 year only.

Send Check/Money Order to: **CounterPunch, P.O. Box 228, Petrolia, CA 95558**
Canada add $12.50 per year postage. Others outside US add $17.50 per year.

Visit our website for more information: **www.counterpunch.org**

I, Claud:
Memoirs of a
Subversive

By Claud Cockburn

Foreword by Alexander Cockburn

The legendary memoirs of British radical journalist Claud Cockburn are sardonic, hilarious, and filled with rich historical detail. They tell the story of an Oxford-educated Communist who rubbed elbows with everyone from Al Capone to Charles de Gaulle; reported on the Wall Street crash and, from Berlin, on the rise of Hitler; enlisted in the Republican militia in the Spanish Civil War. From London *Times* correspondent to founder-editor of The Week, (prime model for I.F. Stone's Weekly), to Foreign Editor of the *Daily Worker* to sometime editor and senior trouble-maker at *Private Eye* in the 1960s, Cockburn witnessed many of the twentieth century's most important events. He shares his insights into politics and journalism with explosively funny and brilliantly written style.

Available early in 2010 from CounterPunch.org and AK Press
Call 1-800-840-3683
$19.95

Born Under a Bad Sky

By Jeffrey St. Clair

"Movement reporting on a par with Mailer's Armies of the Night"—Peter Linebaugh, author of *Magna Carta Manifesto* and *The Many-Headed Hydra*.

These urgent dispatches are from the frontlines of the war on the Earth. Gird yourself for a visit to a glowing nuclear plant in the backwoods of North Carolina, to the heart of Cancer Alley where chemical companies hide their toxic enterprise behind the dark veil of Homeland Security, and to the world's most contaminated place, the old H-bomb factory at Hanford, which is leaking radioactive poison into the mighty Columbia River.

With unflinching prose, St. Clair confronts the White Death in Iraq, the environmental legacy of a war that will keep on killing decades after the bombing raids have ended. He conjures up the environmental villains of our time, from familiar demons like James Watt and Dick Cheney to more surprising figures, including Supreme Court Justice Stephen Breyer (father of the cancer bond) and the Nobel laureate Al Gore, whose pieties on global warming are sponsored by the nuclear power industry. The mainstream environmental movement doesn't escape indictment. Bloated by grants from big foundations, perched in high-rent office towers, leashed to the neoliberal politics of the Democratic Party, the big green groups have largely acquiesced to the crimes against nature that St. Clair so vividly exposes.

All is not lost. From the wreckage of New Orleans to the imperiled canyons of the Colorado, a new green resistance is taking root. The fate of the grizzly and the ancient forests of Oregon hinge on the courage of these green defenders. This book is also a salute to them.